SOUTHERLY

Volume 64, Number 2
2004

THE JOURNAL OF THE ENGLISH ASSOCIATION, SYDNEY

HALSTEAD PRESS

CONTENTS

→ SOUTHERLY →

THE JOURNAL OF THE ENGLISH ASSOCIATION
VOLUME 64, NUMBER 2

EDITORS: DAVID BROOKS & NOEL ROWE
www.arts.usyd.edu.au/Arts/departs/english/southerly

GUEST EDITORS FOR THIS ISSUE
NICOLETTE STASKO AND MARK TREDININCK

COVER IMAGE: Vicki King
COVER DESIGN AND LAYOUT: Vivien Valk
PRINTING: Ligare

EDITORIAL ADVISERS: Michael Brennan, John Hawke, Brian Kiernan, Mabel Lee, Vivian Smith, Ken Stewart, Helen Tiffin, Penny van Toorn, James Tulip, Elizabeth Webby, G. A. Wilkes.

EDITORIAL ASSISTANTS: Pat Skinner, Greg McLaren, Michelle Weisz, Audrey Grey.

→ CONTRIBUTIONS →

Whenever possible, contributions are paid for at higher than the following minimum rates: articles $150; poems $60; reviews $100; short stories $150. Academic papers in *Southerly* are refereed. Material should be accompanied by return postage and sent to:

Editors, *Southerly*
Department of English, Woolley Building A20
University of Sydney NSW 2006, Australia

PUBLISHED BY Halstead Press, 2005
300/3 Smail Street, Broadway, NSW 2007, Australia
Tel: +61 (2) 9211 3033   Fax: +61 (2) 9211 3677
halstead@halsteadpress.com.au

→ SUBSCRIPTION RATES →

Annual Subscriptions include three issues and should be paid in Australian dollars to the publisher.

Individuals: Australia $58 incl. GST; Overseas AU$69.
Institutions: Australia $79 incl. GST; Overseas AU$89.

ENGLISH ASSOCIATION: Subscriptions include *Southerly* and should be paid to:
The Hon. Secretary, English Association
Box 91 Wentworth Building, University of Sydney, Sydney NSW 2006

BACK ISSUES: Volumes I–VI (1939–45) are available from: Johnson Reprint Corporation 111 Fifth Avenue, New York 3, New York USA.

ISSUE AND ARTICLE COPIES: 16mm and 35mm microfilm; and 105mm microfiche are available from: University Microfilms, 300 N. Zeeb Road, Ann Arbor MI 48106 USA.

This publication is assisted by The Australia Council, the Australian Government's arts advisory and support organisation, the New South Wales Ministry for the Arts, and the School of English, Art History, Film and Media, University of Sydney.

ISSN 0038-373   Print Post No. PP255003/05393   ISBN 1 920 831 08 8

4

EDITORIAL

The core of this issue of *Southerly* arises out of an event, Watermark, a festival of nature writing that took place at Camden Haven on the north coast of New South Wales in October 2003; and it is dedicated, as that festival was, to landscape and literature. Much of what you'll read here was born at that muster or is the work of people who were there, at an event that may help found a stronger Australian literature of place. "Watermarks" gathers together prose and poetry that render the more than merely human world. It also offers up some pieces of ecocriticism—literary criticism that takes nature seriously, that reads works of words as if their natural history really counted.

Robert Gray's poem "Joan Eardley in Catterline" and John Hughes' essay "What Remains" describe a kind of artistic engagement with landscape that lies at the heart of what the nature writer, like the visual artists Gray and Hughes, considers and attempts. In Gray's poem, Eardley's painting is a kind of judo, which lets the sea and sky compose the work out of the painter's dynamic, embodied and imaginal engagement with it. The painter sets her easel down in the water, in the storm. She gets wet. She paints her own death not only with paint but with the storm. What she paints is the storm and the bay and herself within nature. In John Hughes' essay we meet another painter, John Wolseley, whose landscape painting is made as much by the burned heath, his subject, as by the artist himself. It is "drawn together." It is the result of the artist's dance in and with a heath, with fire, with the world.

This drawing together is what many of the writers in this collection attempt. For works of words do not merely name things; they do not merely represent them. As Margaret Somerville puts it, words can make her body a membrane upon which some pieces of a place, to which she surrenders and which surrender themselves to her, may resonate. Her body can be a register of the world; her work can be what that rhythmic encounter gives rise to. In writing, too, we can dance with places. For writing is patterned sound; it is, like a place on earth, composed of cadences and intervals, of energies in relationship. And what you may hear in some of these pieces is the music of some places and the rhythm of how these writers were moved by them.

Scott Slovic's essay describes the enterprise of nature writing— "environmental literature", reminding us that what we are talking about here is a literature, nothing less—as something profoundly political. Its task is to find new ways to reanimate the language we use for landscapes so as to reanimate those landscapes in our minds and in the discourses of politics, law-making and everyday life, so that, in turn, we might preserve something of their dignity in the face of the destruction we continue to wage. "How can we save what we do not love?" Aldo Leopold once asked; and "How can we love what we do not know?" Nature writing is a literature of intimacy with places, with country. In many ways, through many devices, it reminds us of our embeddedness in the world, so that we might live here rightly; so that we may save the places that house us. If this literature helps save the land, it will be because it discovers the words and models the behaviours for practising a more loving, listening kind of belonging upon the earth.

But we live here on a continent where such a land ethic has been practised for many thousands of years; where land has been held sacred and served intelligently. "Are we capable of learning from others in our midst?" Nonie Sharp asks in "Reflections on Water." "Does non-indigenous Australia have the humility, the awareness, 'the listening ear,' to learn from Aboriginal people today?" And, I would add, from the land itself, the teacher of Aboriginal people all this long time.

There are non-Indigenous writers—dwellers—who have let the land and its first people school them. Eric Rolls, patron of Watermark and author of two short lyric essays you'll find here, is one. Judith Wright, whose work for reconciliation with country and between peoples, and whose activism and art are recalled in several pieces here, was another. Tom Griffiths points to some pastoral narratives, like Alice Duncan-Kemp's, which have not made it into the national consciousness, and from which it is clear that, while elsewhere the land was being stolen and ravaged, some settlers had the courage to listen to the land and its "landlords." There have always been some, among the colonisers—pastoralists and writers—who have allowed the land to take possession of them, their bodies and their words. Australia already has an astonishing poetic tradition of the lyric apprehension of place as the poetry of Robert Adamson, Judith Beveridge and others in this volume illustrates. And, in the tradition of *Southerly*, we also have new voices such as Illinda Markova and Charlie Ward to add to this chorus. The expressiveness of country that began to sound out of our poetry in the 1960s has been slower in reaching our prose. But this volume is proof that our sentences and paragraphs are growing more sclerophyll by the year: that we are listening to the land—essaying its very nature.

Mark Tredinnick

ANTHONY LAWRENCE

SPRING EQUINOX

Having heard her speak, and then mime a description
of how she intends to balance a brown, still warm,
free-range egg on its tapering end, I practise alone
with a white, thin-shelled egg some battery hen

had abandoned to its tray on a row of death.
All attempts to have it stand are met
with the muted, rolling sound of shell on polished wood
and then silence before the crack and flow

of yolk so pale, you can almost see and smell
the hormone-injected gruel that shaped it.
And now she is ready. She has no degree from the School
of Ancient Wisdom. She has not professed

to having found a way to tame the laws
of gravity or its sisters Air and Breaking Ground.
She tells me it is only now, in the equally weighted light
and dark of the Spring Equinox, that an egg

can achieve its own equilibrium
under cover of a wind-governed season where, like an obelisk
seen from a distance, it will appear to have been
upended and planted for good, unknown reasons.

Before she begins, her instructions are clear:
no music or heated discussion, no movement near
the blackwood table she has chosen, and as for the hen
responsible for this fine, tactile specimen, she can

maintain her vigil, one-eyed and flicking through
the cartoon frames her head makes at the window.
She leans in and over the egg as though warming it
with her breath and the long dark panels

of her insulating hair. Her fingertips make a cage,
allowing the egg enough room to move until
movement diminishes and then stops, and when
her hands rise and angle away, as if two spiders

in the cool, remarkable joinery of their skins
had been startled from copying each other,
the egg demands and receives my attention.
I inspect it, as close as my breathing

and loose clothing will allow. She joins me,
saying at dusk the egg will topple, cold
and out of kilter with the spell-binding work of the world.
With the mountain drained of perspective and light,

the egg falls down, and rocks to settle on the wood.
When I hold it, something wrought from pure
amazement forms, dissolves, then reforms
in the quartering chambers of my heart.

ELAINE VAN KEMPEN

WATERMARK

WATERMARK: a pattern swirled in paper; a pattern marked on land by the swirling ripples and waves of water; an international nature-writers' and readers' muster that made strong impressions and waves in the lives of all who participated.

That Watermark had its genesis in a whisper, at first barely heard. In 1994, Eric Rolls and I moved to live in the Camden Haven on the mid-north coast of New South Wales. For Eric it meant "fishing as a reward for a good day's writing" but I had no idea what it meant for me. And then I heard a voice: it seemed that the place itself was whispering to me. Eric has, it said, unwittingly joined a local literary tradition. Another joined in, they became louder, and I went out to see whose voices they were.

I found Henry Kendall (1839–82) who came to live in a village called Camden Haven in 1875 and stayed until 1881, just a year before he died. That village later changed its name to Kendall in his honour and the Camden Haven became the collective name for the villages that stretch from Camden Head on the edge of the Pacific Ocean, through Kendall, to the plateau near Comboyne where the Camden Haven River rises.

Kendall came here after a disastrous time in a life of disastrous times. After the death of their beloved daughter Araluen in 1870, he was estranged from his wife Charlotte and his two sons for nearly six years. He broke down and was consigned, for a period, to Gladesville Insane Asylum. But, after he came to Camden Haven, he and Charlotte reunited happily in 1876 and another little boy and two more little girls were born to them. He wrote some of his best poetry here.

Despite the influence of the Victorian Romanticism of the day, Kendall wrote with a rare Australianness. A. G. Stephens spoke later of his "rare gift of seeing, and hearing, and feeling, and describing our Australian wilderness".

In 1942 Douglas Stewart published Eric's poem "Death Song of Mad Bush Shepherd", written when he was fifteen years old, on the Red Page of that lovely big old *Bulletin*. Immediately picked up and broadcast by both the ABC and the BBC, it was hailed as the first wholly Australian poem: it could have come from nowhere else. Australian nature writing began with the poets.

Kylie Tennant (1912–88) came to live in the Camden Haven during World War II when her husband became head teacher of Laurieton Primary School. She made friends with a farmer, Ernie Metcalf, who built a slab hut for her to write in on land he owned beside the sea at Diamond Head. Kylie's "Lost Haven", published in 1946, evoked the spirit of this place. "The Man on the Headland", published in 1971, evoked Ernie's spirit as well. Place writing at its best.

Now I knew whose voices I was hearing. To them my mind added more Australian voices and others in the English language, all of them spiritual descendants of Gilbert White and Henry David Thoreau, all of them celebrating a literature of nature and place that deserved to be more widely read, more widely heard.

When a small group of people (of which I was one) took over the former Camden Head Pilot Station under the auspices of the local adult and community education organisation, it provided a potential venue for the nature writing event that was building in my mind.

Henry had been celebrated sporadically in the village of Kendall since the bi-centenary of European arrival in Australia, Kylie had been recognised by the renovation of her writing hut, now within a National Park. During the refurbishment of the Pilot Station cottage and boathouse, the committee began annual events in their names.

Other writers—friends—visiting Eric and me found that they were giving readings and talks under the banksias near the boathouse. England's Roger Deakin (Waterlog) claimed the title of Pilot Writer when he shared the first gig there with Eric and a determined, raucous Little Wattle-Bird.

Mark Tredinnick came to stay with us and was regaled with unformed plans for an event that knew only that it was to be neither a conference nor a festival. Exactly what it was to be was elusive, but he understood. After all, he'd come to ask Eric to contribute to an anthology of nature writing. Mark became the Pilot Resident in the newly refurbished cottage and he was very quickly joined by Richard Nelson, visiting from Alaska. We were encouraged by their enthusiasm and generosity, they introduced us to other writers.

For eighteen months the regular lunches at our blackwood dining table—monthly, fortnightly, then weekly—enjoyed by four women, Mavis Barnes, Andrina Dawson, Lyndal Coote and me, were spiced with inspiration and leavened by very hard work. And we laughed a lot. Lyndal's meticulous record keeping and enthusiastic communication with writers made her all but indispensable. Eric shared our lunch, provided advice, lent his name to all we did and then went back to his writing.

Bernadette Hince and Nicholas Drayson spent two weeks in residence at the Pilot Station and became so engaged with our plans that, when the time came, they came back to assist.

Watermark International Nature Writers' Muster began with an informal dinner on Monday 6 October 2003 and ended with Herb Wharton's wonderful Henry Kendall Oration at a luncheon on Saturday 11. On the first day participants met at the Pilot Station to become grounded with sessions that considered What Place is This? and Whose Place is This?, they explored Washhouse Beach and walked the Flower Bowl circuit in the adjacent Kattang Nature Reserve. We had rashly promised whales; they arrived on cue.

Rosemarie Piontek joined us in the last few weeks and brought calm organisation into the essential daily good food and wine activities of the muster. USA poet, Laurie Kutchins, dubbed us the Goddesses and the name stuck, except for Herb Wharton who prefers "goodliness to godliness". Herb calls us the Goodesses.

The Muster moved to Kendall School of Arts, just up the road from where Henry worked for Fagan's timber mill. Sessions such as "Watering a New Crop—writing for young people", "Pools of Wisdom—women's words", "Laying down the lore—what role for literature?", "A Novel Approach to Nature", "Living the Land", "Indigenous People's Knowledge", drew capacity audiences. Martin Flanagan spoke passionately at a literary dinner. The Camden Haven Choir sang "coral" music. We launched books—Mark Tredinnick's *A Place on Earth* (UNSW Press) and Peter Grant's *Habitat Garden* (ABC Books), and we sold books—$10,000 worth! ASLE ANZ was born of a cross-Tasman marriage.

Writers came from the United States, Japan and England, other writers and readers came from all over Australia and from New Zealand. It is their prerogative to comment on Watermark:

It was simply the best of any meeting of people in which I've been involved of the scale of conference, symposium, colloquium. It was also by far the best of anything I have been to in the writers' and readers' festival category. (Geoff Park, New Zealand)

Since the closing moments of Watermark, I've been carrying a kind of euphoria around with me, brought on by the remarkable energy, engagement and excitement that was created there. Here in America, we've had a number of fairly large gatherings centered around nature writing, and I've participated in quite a few of them. But Watermark was unprecedented in my experience. (Richard Nelson, Alaska)

My invitation to Watermark will be remembered as one of the most important events in my writing life. (Patrice Newell, Australia)

The more I think about the magic you wove at Watermark, the more apt the title Goddesses seems. I booked… thinking that if the muster wasn't my bag I could go home…. I think Richard Nelson was the first hook when he asked of the magpie, what sort of wind could create a bird like that? By lunch on day one I knew I couldn't head home early. Many things stay with me… the passion and utter humility of the writers, the diversity of interests and skills of everyone there, the right-ness of Pete Hay's and others' advocacy of activism in nature writing. (Dael Allison, Australia)

Congratulations on the work of all the goddesses—in making Watermark so richly rewarding as a social and intellectual event. (Tom Griffiths, Australia)

Know that your accomplishments were/are significant and poignant, and I believe will reverberate long after the Muster itself. Know that I am thinking of you all… and utterly marveling at the impact of the Muster. (Laurie Kutchins, USA)

Watermark will be held biennially, the October 2005 muster is being planned now. The Watermark Literary Society has been incorporated to administer future events and an anonymous donation will sponsor a biennial Nature Writing Fellowship to be offered to an Emerging Writer in the opposite year to Watermark. The literary tradition is secure. The Camden Haven will continue to celebrate literature of nature and place.

HERB WHARTON

NAMATJIRA

Albert Namatjira
a man of ancient race
educated in Dream Time Law
the earth, mother, father, everything.

He broke a white man's law
Some trivial little matter.
He gave his people wine,
an alien's racial crime it was
in a land his elders owned since
Dream Time

Namatjira went to prison.
Inhuman was this judgement
and a broken heart he died.
His studio was Australia's red heart,
rugged eroded lonely ranges
with ever changing colours.

Namatjira put them all on canvas
the stately majestic
Ghost gums he painted,
Namatjira, he stood tall.

Now the world can view
the scenes that Namatjira painted.
His painting and his name,
like his dreamtime legends,
they will always be remembered.

For some things you gave the world
Albert Namtajira
you will always be remembered.

TELL ME A STORY
Looking at picture of old man on wall

Old man form the dreamtime
tell me a story
of your legends and lores
or tell me of nature
and a mother called earth.

Who taught you a medicine
How to make fire
Who was builder taught you to fish
With traps made of stone.

Genetics you knew of
Controlling of birth
Breeding and marriage
What was right meat
What was taboo
Who was doctor made all these rules.

The shaping of grindstone
For milling of flour
Designing of boomerang
Woomerra and spear
Who hold the patient
Old man from the past.

When lacking in calories
dirt rich in vitamins
from anthill you ate
who was dietician told you do that
detoxin the poison
from berries and roots
who was the chemist
Taught you do that.

The corroborees you dance
movements and step
who wrote the script.
the drumming and clacking of sticks
the sounds of horn made from wood
who was musician
Old man on the wall.

The painting in caves
and peckings on stone
who was historian
recorded all that.

Alas only silence
from old man on wall
his secrets (old dreamtime)
lay hidden
in depth of the soil.

Old tribalman from dreamtime past
you knew of nature's secrets
you worshipped mother earth
men trying to learn today
Things you knew ten thousand years ago.

With rocket ships now aimed at Mars
Men have walked upon the moon
Yet still secrets of your dreamtime
and hope of future races
all lie in mother earth.

NONIE SHARP

REFLECTION ON WATER

I. WELL-SPRINGS: WATER IN THE RELIGIOUS AND ARTISTIC IMAGINATION

The smell of damp dark earth. We are awaiting the return of the lyre-bird to her mound. Sherbrooke Falls, magical place of my early memories. The fall of water, crystal clear; the stones. Bright green moss, fern gullies, straight tall trees, reaching to the sky. It is the 1930s. I am a small child sometimes walking the track, sometimes being carried.

My father drinks the clear water in cupped hands. Like receiving communion bread, I reflect later. Sherbrooke forest is situated in my child mind as a place of transcendent beauty. The altars of moss-covered rocks are like stepping stones towards a spiritual presence.

The Nature poets of the Romantic period stirred that imagination. In "Nun's Well, Brigham", Wordsworth brings together the purity of the spring and the Spirit that inhabits that place and makes it sacred: "... round the limestone cell/ Of the pure spring.../ A tender Spirit broods— the pensive Shade/ Of ritual honours to this Fountain paid."

In the Judaeo-Christian tradition, in the Vedic tradition and in others, waters are *fons et origo*, spring and origin of life. The word *fons* means a spring, and fountain is derived from the word *fontana*. The waters precede every form and support every creation; they are living and life-giving. Genesis 2 records that "The Spirit of God moved upon the face of the waters"; and in due course He "gathered together into one place the waters and let the dry land appear". So the waters have a religious valorisation. Encountering a spring or spring-fed well stirs a sense of returning to and re-entering the time of creation; it is also supporting a new creation.

In enshrining a spiritual, an otherworldly power, pure waters carry healing properties especially those springing from the earth or mountain-side. These beliefs lie deep within many cultures—as in the legend of King Bladud, the mythical founder of Bath in England. Shelley's beautiful poem adapts this legend in which a banished leper stumbles upon a warm cleft of rocks "through which the might of healing springs is poured".

More than 20 years ago I became aware of Mircea Eliade's understanding of eternal return, his insight into the sacredness of water across many cultures. He helped me to understand how water became so tightly woven into the fabric of our lives, our beliefs, our sensibilities. Water flows, it is living: it inspires, it heals, it prophesies. Spring water and fountains display power, life, perpetual renewal. Water then isn't *just* water; its creative and life-giving qualities bind together the needs of the body with those of the spirit. In the Judaeo Christian tradition bread is the staff of life; water is its fount.

No wonder then that across places and times, cults of springs and streams have flourished. Springs, natural fountains and watercourses have been surrounded and imbued with supernatural powers from ancient times. Homer refers to cults of rivers and Hesiod mentions how sacrifices were made when crossing a river. In places where Christianity put down roots it assimilated many pre-existing water cults. In the sixth century St Gregory of Tours noted men making offerings to a lake there, whereupon on the fourth day of the rite a storm arose followed by rain. So a priest built a church there to encourage men to make offerings to God and forget about the lake and its deities. There is no doubt that Christianity went on to make a symbolic association between the effervescent purity of fountain and spring with the healing and redemptive power of the Divine as in the hymn to Jehovah: "Open now the crystal fountain/ Whence the healing stream doth flow..."

II. Transition: Water as a Scarce Commodity

In the way I've been describing, water came to be embedded in everyday and in spiritual life. It was part of life's majesty and spiritual potency, and it was everyday. It renewed the body and the spirit. It became so tightly woven into the fabric of human life that its presence was taken for granted. That is, it became *a cultural* rather than just a physical phenomenon. Its life-giving function is something we leave unquestioned; its meanings are interwoven with what it is to be human. The presence of water in the great rivers of Australia was not a matter for debate. Water was flowing in these rivers. All this has changed.

Over 60 years since I took my first steps into the lyre-bird forests of the hills northeast of Melbourne, much of the religious, emotional and artistic meaning and attraction of water has disappeared. Today the meaning given to water has shrunk: water is now prosaic. Overwhelmingly it is just a resource—inseparable from the essence of life, but simply a resource nonetheless. Moreover, and this is connected, where once it was taken for granted—there like air for everyone to share in—it is now not only a resource but a scarce one world wide. As everyone knows, water has always been scarce at certain times and places; yet its current scarcity is ongoing, critical and worsening. Indeed, a world water crisis is recognised as a threat to the existence of future generations and scarily—a likely cause of future wars.

Since ancient times, water was taken to be like air—free for everyone to share in. The classical Roman jurists—Seneca, Ovid, Virgil, Cicero—proclaimed that like air and sun, water is a common gift of nature to all mankind. Today, the ominous threat of permanent scarcity is accompanied by a third change. Water has become a thing, a marketable commodity. You can see this on the Murray or the Darling. As historian Heather Goodall records, along the Darling you hear the haunting words: "The river runs backwards ... when they turn on the pumps!" Who? The cotton irrigators with 36 inch pipes.

Why, one may ask, talk about what's gone? Why return to the source as it were? Does what held good for most of human history continue to hold an attraction to us?

Because we know or sense that water had a thicker, more embodied meaning (if one can say that about a liquid) to view and experience in the imagination what went before is like visiting a sanctuary. Are there elements of a nostalgic search to reinstate the spiritual. Something akin to the yearning for the purity of unspoiled forests? Or is something more happening?

III. STILL RIVERS?

A few decades ago there were some people in Australia with a clear awareness of a growing environmental crisis. The poet Judith Wright, environmentalist Eric Rolls, others too had more than a premonition that water would feature more and more in a growing crisis of Nature. Bruce Davidson's *Australia Wet or Dry* and Jock Marshall's book with the unequivocal title *The Great Extermination: A Guide to Australia's Cupidity, Wickedness and Waste* stand out. Now a few solo singers warning us of impending danger—water crisis, river crisis, redgum forest crisis—have been joined by a choir of voices with new and powerful verses and refrains. Have we the foresight, the humility and commitment to engage afresh with Nature?

READING AND CONSULTING WITH THE SEA

We are travelling from Mer, the largest of the three Murray Islands, Torres Strait to Waier, a dark enchanting rocky outcrop. It's 1978, and I'm a new chum. He keeps looking around and turning the boat. We seem to be travelling along roads in the sea. Above the noise of the motor he's telling me names of places in the sea. I can't make out where he's pointing. But later I find that the Meriam follow seamarks as well as landmarks. In the shallows he idles the motor. Facing a cavernous rockface of this turreted rock castle, he speaks loudly in his language. It's as if he's negotiating with someone. Who? The ancestral spirits. Koge—that's one of his 19 names—speaks with feeling about his ancestral lands and seas. He belongs to that locale associated with the southwest wind, to turtle and mackerel totems, and his words about these—his inheritance—are emotionally charged. "My grandfather took me to this place and said: 'Here are your lands, here are your seas, here are your reefs…'"

It's a week later now. Three of us are sitting beside a beach at Mer. "When Pleiades begins to rise this is a sign to the gardener to plant certain yams before the first rains of the wet season." The Pleiades' rising means it's good for voyaging to their neighbours on the PNG and Australian coasts. Similar knowledge to the ancient Greeks. The moon and sun cycles are part of the Meriam calendar: "Use new moon for plants that bear fruit on the surface, full moon for plants that grow down." Meriam knowledge of natural cycles is immense; but neither a grab bag nor just encyclopaedic knowledge. It follows the often complex relationships between different cycles; that's why they can say, when it's a good year for wongai, the red plum they share with the TS pigeon, it'll be a good year for the turtle egg laying season. Or, more immediately, "When the shark constellation rises this is the time turtles come."

Their lives move in step not only with seasons, with lunar and daily cycles, but with the complex rhythmic set of arrangements continually reborn in new tides that have their own life stages, each of which varies according to wind or season.

No wonder the elder I am sitting beside says "I read nature for my book…" And "reading" the land or the sea is an experience of deep aesthetic emotion. *We are on the big hill of Mer now listening to the sea. "You hear that murmuring, that's the sound of the sea breaking on the Great Barrier Reef." I listen. It sounds sort of uncanny. Their words for its distant murmur echo the sound itself. Maiso mir, murmuring words or talk. "Wooo...like a drum. This is the sea speaking to you. The murmur can tell you lots of things. 'It's going to be calm weather.' If it makes a louder noise a big wind is coming. A bad time for voyaging." The "voice of the sea" is echoed in the sound of the trumpet or triton shell blown all over the Torres Strait Islands to make important announcements.*

From life to death the person, the group, the locale are continually recreated as sentient and sensuous. Importantly, their face-to-face experiences are carried with them in memory and in their practices. The feelings experienced—especially of sharing—is retained. Often these are many-layered. I am sitting with my sister Dolly, and it is southwest time. Our season. A frigate bird flies overhead. She cries. "Why are you crying?" "Because the frigate bird makes me think of my father; this bird was one of his totems." She breaks into a song of the southwest wind bringing the frigate bird to her home island. That knowledge, given in song, is also a statement about rights to her land and sea. Four themes run through what I've sketched so briefly about the Meriam and many Aboriginal coastal peoples. 1.Their lives are founded upon and recreate face to face groups and persons. 2.Their knowledge carries with it their feelings and emotions. 3.Their lives are set within natural cycles. 4.Consequently, their knowledge is layered, building up its complexity from the relations between the various cycles and events within them. They read and consult with Nature and Nature is not linear.

RESONANCE? THE POETIC IMAGINATION

Are there points of contact between indigenous knowledge and the poetic imagination as it has developed in European tradition? And why do I ask this? I'm interested in truths with which non-indigenous Australia has lost touch; truths which, in an imperilled world may help us to think afresh.

In an address to women writers in 1980, the poet Judith Wright spoke of the poetic imagination as a particular way of looking at the world. In encouraging women writers to nurture their poetic faculties, she pointed to several qualities of the poetic imagination that I think resonate with indigenous people's ways of living and knowing the land, the sea and one another. She mentions Susanne Langer's "Poetic Creation" essay where poetry is seen as formulating "the appearance of feeling, of subjective experience...." Very importantly, Wright herself says that the poetic vision is inimical to the linear-thinking that lies behind "the ideal of Material Progress". (I must say that Judith herself lived a life of "comparative poverty"—her own words.) She explains how the poetic imagination includes and implies a "re-creation of personal, group and national relationships".

IN OUR TIME... ENGAGING AFRESH WITH NATURE

In the past children sang with pride "I love a sunburnt country", Dorothy McKellar's song about the wide brown land in its contradictory vicissitudes. Today Australia has become browner, drier, saltier, less diverse.... Many people grieve for the country and are moved to ask the question: Are we capable of learning from others in our midst and from our own past? Does non-indigenous Australia have the humility, the awareness, "the listening ear", to learn from Aboriginal people today? A decade ago Eric Rolls noted how every year we are learning more about Aboriginal management of lands, rivers and seas; something of the subtle beauty of their Australia. My sense of the people of the land and sea in northern coastal Australia is one of an elegant, rich and sophisticated knowledge repertoire, one in which people actually live and get their cues from celestial and earthly flows and patterns. I am reminded of Barry Lopez's words in *Arctic Dreams*: how invisible fibres seem to tie Inuit people with their landscape.

In his 2003 essay, environmentalist Tim Flannery locates the degradation of the environment in the social and cultural assumptions that guide the way we engage with the world. What he doesn't do himself is to engage with post-settlement and contemporary indigenous land and water management in post-*Mabo* Australia. Yet indigenous people's way of reconciling and consulting with Nature may help people like Tim or me or you to re-imagine how we might engage afresh with the natural and social world. Their way has for instance, caught the imagination of the Wentworth Group: Aboriginal caring for country is chosen as one of its four principles. More recklessly Germaine Greer sees Australia's resurrection in becoming a hunter-gatherer nation. To me her proposal is both fanciful and presumptuous: like the people she criticises, Germaine does not reveal herself as someone aware of the ancient depth, the intricacies, the profundity of Aboriginal knowledge, which shapes them as hunter-gatherers.

**

If we could just reorganise ourselves a little, we might spend less time on individually oriented betterment as defined by the market and more on the creation and re-creation of interrelationships between persons and groups founded upon reciprocity. I think that that is what Judith Wright was getting at.

Works Cited

Tim Flannery, "Beautiful Lies: Population and Environment in Australia", *Quarterly Essay* 9 (2003): 1–73, esp. 4–16, 64–69.

Heather Goodall, "The River Runs Backwards", in T. Bonyhady & T. Griffiths, eds., *Words for Country: Landscape and Language in Australia* (Sydney: University of New South Wales Press, 2002) 31–51.

Germaine Greer, "Whitefella Jump Up: The Shortest Way to Nationhood", *Quarterly Essay* 11 (2003): 1–78, esp. 77–78.

Judith Wright, "Women and Writing", address to Women Writers Congress, Melbourne, 1980, in Judith Wright, *Going on Talking* (Springwood, NSW: Butterfly Books, 1992) 24.

DINAH HAWKEN

THE POLITICAL LAKE

1.
Odd the chance
that I am here on the edge
of Lake Geneva during the G8
watching coots.

She is sitting on the grassy
beginnings of a nest
on the transom of Romantico
in a dream producing chicks.

He is coming and going with sticks.
Helicopters carry men
from one summit to another.

The lake hosts everyone who comes
to it. It is as neighbourly
as a saint. But there is a limit
to so much giving.

In a dance of homage to the tops
of trees and to a Swiss flag
lifting: a flock of darting swallows.

Flapping like a canvas, galloping
like horses, I hear swans
over the silent lake.

I can't see the lake for the birds.
You can't see the wood for the trees.
We can't see the world for the people.

2.
The people—we are shown—
are suffering. We can't see life
for the suffering. Our hands are bound
and our feet are bound
by this long, narrow tape
of suffering.

Cynicism. Spin. On the edge
of Lake Geneva. Weak words
for spiked drinks that lead to nothing
but broken glass and
half-broken bones.

And don't talk to me
about the violence done to you
while you are taking so much
of that young woman's blood. Look.
It is all over your face, your hands.
Your hospital gown.

But who am I to speak out?
I don't give my blood
and I am sheltered and, so far,
sane.

Our gestures represent ourselves
the way poplar leaves
flickering over the willing lake
represent the wind.

Today my instinct is to stay here
watching other creatures
building and re-building
their floating nests.

3.
Because water is simpler
than a bird, or a tree
or a woman

I could allow this poem
to become a bowl
for which water has a use
and an affinity:

I could tell you
that a river
with its tributaries
enters and fills the same lake

that a river flows from
towards its estuary and leaves:

I could tell you
that the three words

fluency, depth, luminosity

are

to the beauty I see
what the volume of water
in the bowl is
to the volume of the lake:

but I don't need
to tell a soul
about the need for water

—or the need for light
on water.   Reflection
puts no weight on a lake.

OUYANG YU (TRANSLATOR)

POEMS FROM THE CHINESE

YEAR OF RETURN
Du Fu (712–770)

birds are whiter against a limpid river
flowers are about to burst into flame on a green hill
this spring looks like it's taking leave again
but when will it be my year of return?

BOAT SONG IN ORCHID CREEK
Dai Shulun (732–789)

a cool moon, like a brow, hanging over willow bay
yuezhong mountain seen as in a mirror
peach flower rain in orchid creek for three days
brings carp up the midnight beach

MT FUJI
Huang Zunxian (1848–1905)

rising tall on itself into the sky
the lotus peak surging out of the eastern waves
its snow two thousand five hundred years old
remains unmelted and white

PUSHING THE WINDOW OPEN
Yuan Mei (1716–1798)

bad wind and rain a whole night
my hut remains closed
the mountain, missing me, is so impatient
that he comes in full on my face as soon as i push open the
window

CROSSING THE HAN RIVER
Li Pin (818?–876)

i've heard nothing from beyond the mountain
from last winter till this spring
as i near my home i grow so timid
that i dare not ask anyone a question

NO POINT LEANING AGAINST THE RAILING ALONE
Li Yu (ca. 937–978)

a fine rain outside the curtain, the spring at an end
your silk quilt too thin against the early morning cold
forgetting you were a visitor, you wasted money seeking
pleasure

no point leaning against the railing alone, to see endless rivers
and mountains
for it's easy to bid farewell but hard to meet again
with flowing water and fallen flowers, the spring is gone,
heaven and earth

WILL YOU COME BACK?
Wang Wei (ca. 699–761)

after i see you off in the mountain
i close the wooden gate behind me at dusk
the spring grass will turn green next year
but will you come back then?

PETRA WHITE

IDEAS OF ORDER AT POINT LONSDALE

The ageing pier croons and sways,
     a tied-up boat, entirely absorbed
in water's undecided plunk
     against its sides, at any moment
ready to unmire and carry
     out to fields of shadeless glitter, some
scarcely fazeable fishermen;
     and children, twitching in the fresh air,
goose-bumped, beaded with salt water;
     balancing, climbing on the railing,
their faces wholly kaleidoscoped,
     who hurl out an empty line and shout
to a sea-monster half-aroused
     below; but the line flings back again,
a spider fleeing its own web,
     forced by the hide-and-seeking stranger
wind, and the smallest bumps her head
     on the rail and cries. All three watch as
water turns serious, furrowing
     and frowning into its first depths—
hooked parrotfish swing, flashing their
     lively mutilated corpses, fish
after fish seeps through the cloudy
     eye of its brother; sea unfolds its
never-to-be-lifted skirt, the
     children, silenced with real bait, crouch tense
as lovers, fighting off a slow
     descending weariness of no named
inheritance; a deep whale yawn
     like someone's or no-one's tired mother's
drops into early dusk, the boy
     startles, looks out past the others, his
chest puffing out armour, the sock
     slipping round his ankle; and each wave,
with toothless grin and snarling beard,
     rolls in its bed and visibly dreams
of a fish as spry as his hand,
     green as his green eye, arch as his foot.

And each holds fast, none drift, although
     the wide black ships thin to their pin-lights,
and the young moon goes spritzing off
     to haunt another planet: the prize catch,
the salmon that fought so all lines
     tangled, dragged back and forth by the mouth,
lies in a long string bag, slung low
     round the elephant leg of the pier,
forgotten even as dinner,
     alive, pushed by the sea in and out
of shadows, a mascot dancing
     alone, to an old, bleak music of
rising water, its silver scales...
     Stiff in the breeze, the moth-eaten man
near my elbow clings to his rod
     that seems to be steering him home, or
into the shade of a fixed star
     hidden out of sight. Time like a barge
moves in and quietly chafes at
     a last hour's stillness. Some people pass
with murmuring children and clanky
     buckets. He flinches like a hatchling
as trip-traps of feet grow louder
     then suddenly cease, the boards humming
above cold sea. What makes him stay?
     The sea surges on its indigo
as if to shove us back to land;
     but his dilate eye blazes with an
outward-seeking light as ships glide
     in and blow their horns to the houses
nestled behind the cypresses,
     and a bark boat scrubs down to a leaf,
on waters where North creeps behind
     clouds and changes into South. Then a
crab skitters air on the end of
     his line, two eyes looming, wakeful, hot
spears, scrambling to pinch; with a twist
     of the arm he sends it hurtling back.

ERIC ROLLS

WHAT PLACE IS THIS

ONE OF THE MARVELS of a writer's life is its unexpectedness. Days never pass in dreary procession. The writing itself is a joy because the senses are heightened. You seem to be up there somewhere looking down. Words drop on you, and flow through your fingers onto the page, and you welcome them as gifts from the unknown. The imagination must always be ready, its receptors open. This discipline is sometimes interrupted. The snail mail, the email, the fax, the telephone jab you with offers that can not always be refused. Within reasonable expectations, a writer is public property. What demands are reasonable varies from writer to writer. My obligations do not amount to answering the telephone.

We came here unexpectedly. I believe that all the great things in life are the result of snatching opportunity. Odds must be weighed, but a planned life is an accountant's life, devoid of sudden joys. Credit and debit give life a false balance. Since I was a child I've regarded life as an adventure. And the more you know, the better you can experience it. I would not order anything that has happened to me differently. I've led an extraordinarily exciting life, I've always been singularly lucky, mostly I think because I've never been afraid to do something new. And two marvellous women often pointed out directions I had not thought of.

Food and wine lifted us out of the mediocrity of the 1950s. Interesting food is essential to a good life. It carries the same wonderment, it demands the same intensity of imaginative preparation as sex. With my first wife, Joan, I learnt French and Chinese cooking. We grew all our own meat, we found the glorious spritzig German Rieslings that sadly are not made for export anymore. They are drunk at home by old-fashioned vignerons in the Rhein valley.

When Elaine came we added all sorts of Asian and Italian dishes, available ingredients were changing with the population. And Elaine brought a big blackwood dining table that glows with the marvellous talk and superb meals we've had around it. That table demands respect. Only when every other table plus a bed or two are loaded do we dare sort books and papers on it. We can feel the table cringe. It is only happy with platters of food and good wine.

How did we come to live in the Camden Haven? We were on our way to Lismore where I was to talk at the Southern Cross University. When it got dark we decided to drive on. The lights of a tractor reveal a different world, since most animals ignore them and life goes on normally. A paddock by night is fascinating to watch, but arcs of bitumen illuminated by a car's headlights make a lifeless progression. We got out the NRMA guide and found Lobster Pot Motel at North Haven, a place we had never heard of. Well, we stayed there.

Next morning Elaine went for an early walk while I accentuated my talks with red strokes in the motel. She came back excited by North Brother dipping into Watson Taylor Lake and roof of the North Haven Hall following the line of slope. People were pumping yabbies out on the estuary sandbank. "Come and see," she said, and we found a block of land for sale.

During fifty-odd years of inland writing and farming, I'd thought that sometime it would be good to live by the sea and learn to use a boat. European Carp had ruined our freshwater fishing. For years we had gone out on the Barwon River with bait to catch particular fish: the first frost has come, we'll go after cod this trip. So we'd take live feral Crucian Carp, and freshwater crayfish and big larvae of longicorn beetles cut out of Kurrajong trees and we'd come home with three or four beautifully patterned wonders weighing up to twenty kilograms. No more. On one of our last trips we caught one tonne of European Carp, a few hundred of the revolting creatures, and four Yellowbelly.

The block of land had an oyster lease a few metres from the boundary, and they were Sydney Rock Oysters. The awful Pacific Oysters have not yet travelled this far. A Sydney Rock Oyster is a distillation of all the best tastes in the water about it and each water seasons them with its own special flavour. The oysters here are particularly good, and no sulphuric acid from canefields floods down the river to kill them.

North Brother influenced our decision that this was the place to live. It has kindly aspects. People coming home are comforted to see it. "There is the mountain," they say to themselves, "I'm home, I'm safe." Some days it shows individual trees. You can see the black fire-scarred butts that give that name to huge trees on slopes so steep that they were safe from loggers. On other days the mountain is a grey blur, all its attributes hidden. It can be blue, grey, green, splotched with arcs of light and shadow.

In his passage up the coast, James Cook called the three mountains of similar shape the "three brothers", but the Bipai, Nagamba and Bunya people of this area had been telling stories of three brothers thousands of years before Cook. Dooragan is their name for this mountain and they regard it as a protector. Elaine van Kempen wrote its story for National Parks and Wildlife when it became a national park in 1997. It fascinates me because it looks so solid, but like all mountains it is not solid. It flows outwards from the base like a heavy liquid. Admittedly, in a lifetime the distance is infinitesimal, but over a hundred million years it will spread a substantial amount.

Bullock teams worked on top of the mountain, snigging logs to the nearest shoot, one of the steep gullies on the eastern flank that became passageways for logs travelling at high speed from the top to bottom. When the bullocks pulled a log lengthways across the top of the shoot, the driver unhooked them, turned the log butt down into the shoot and let go. If it bumped out of line and hit a rock it might end up as matchsticks.

There are birds here that distinguish the Camden Haven for me. A species I had not seen elsewhere, small grey Mangrove Herons sitting alone silent and hunched like bitterns on the lower rocks of what are arrogantly called "the training walls". Seemingly blue-grey, close-up they reveal an exciting gold patterning on the edges of the wing feathers. It lifts them to new dimensions. They spend hours watching the water, a serious study, not a mere lookout for food. They are more about the estuary than I know.

JOHN I. CAMERON

SANDSTONE STORIES: PLACE WRITING AND EDUCATION

I HAVE THE GOOD FORTUNE to live adjacent to the Blue Mountains National Park with its heath-covered plateaus and deeply incised canyons that protect pockets of temperate coachwood and sassafras rainforest. The jointing pattern in the sandstone ledges in the local Faulconbridge area means that there are many "person-sized" caves and overhangs in the bushland with dark lichen-covered exteriors and intricate honey-coloured wind-carved interiors. The structure of broad exposures of rock and intimate spaces between them has encouraged me to pause during my explorations, to sit quietly and discover the different qualities of each little cave that I encounter.

During the ten years my partner Vicki and I have lived here, I have written more personally about my experiences of place, especially the contrast between our garden and the bushland[1] and have noticed the effect on my teaching practices. Place, writing and education have become increasingly intertwined for me.

I am particularly interested in how the practice of nature writing relates to place-based education because I have long taught undergraduate and postgraduate subjects concerned with the philosophy and practice of place-based education at the University of Western Sydney (UWS). One of my aims with these subjects, each of which has the phrase "sense of place" in its title, has been to facilitate students paying closer attention to their place relationships and enabling them to do so with others. Our whole program in Social Ecology at UWS is run on experiential learning principles, among others, so weekly immersion in a place of their choosing is fundamental to the structure of the subjects, as is a set of readings that includes nature writing.

Students learn to express their emerging responsiveness to their place and its implications. I encourage them to convey their place experiences as directly and in as much detail as possible, to evoke rather than describe, and to reflect on the wider significance of what they have learned from their places. Nature writing has a crucial role in providing exemplars for this expressive act, which is so difficult to master while the power of the experience is so raw.

I work with the students to develop their *practices of place*. Many of them are interested in physical action to sustain a place, such as bush regeneration, fencing off a reserve, or replanting streamside vegetation. To be successful, this requires close observation of the terrain, and developing an understanding of the ecological interrelationships between soil, insect, plant and animal life, and how human actions have affected the local ecology. It involves patiently learning to note down what is actually there, not what one thinks is there, or ought to be there. It is not enough to assume that the same tea-tree understorey continues over the ridge because one would rather not clamber up there to find out.

Learning to pay attention to one's own felt response to a place is an equivalent practice. Just as the eyes (and ears and nose and hands) need to be attuned, so does the heart. It is easy to slip into sentimentalising or romanticising a place rather than carefully noting what one is really feeling. Some nature writing can actually be an obstacle for the place educator at this stage. Students who read accounts of rapturous oneness with Nature are apt to think that this is how they are supposed to feel. I am constantly telling my students on field trips that it is all right not to be in a state of bliss. In fact, I have increasingly discovered that acknowledging displacement or feelings of placelessness can be powerful avenues into place responsiveness (I have benefited greatly from discussions with Vicki on this theme[2]).

There are many other practices that I encourage students to take up—chronicling the natural and human history of a place, keeping a journal and drawing in detailed and non-representational ways, experimenting with Goethe's intuitive science of nature,[3] revisiting childhood place attachments and their significance. I emphasise an understanding of their own cultural practices and how that relates to that of other cultures, notably Aboriginal perspectives on country.

It is interesting to compare these practices with the work of the nature writer. There is much in common, especially in the patient observation, the careful drawing out of the many stories that each place has to tell, the engagement of heart and mind. Thus it is not surprising that good nature writing greatly assists the work of a place educator. The obvious difference is the physical presence of the educator. In the bush, my attentiveness and manner of being speaks more loudly to the students than any words I might utter. Even here, though, the differences can be mitigated by a good writer. Reading Eric Rolls' "A Million Wild Acres",[4] it is easy to feel him walking beside you as he journeys through the Pilliga Scrub describing a forest clearing or changes in the waterways.

I generally characterise place-based education as education concerned with and arising from the experience of a particular place. Although there are limitations to such generalisations, I find it useful to contrast it with outdoor education, which is primarily based on physical challenge, and environmental education, which is primarily knowledge-based. In earlier writings about my teaching practice,[5] I described the work of a place-based educator as holding the creative tension between fostering a depth experience of place and developing critical ecological and social awareness. Without the engagement of the five senses, a felt sense of an ongoing relationship with a particular place at various times of the day and through the changing seasons, and the discovery of its many stories, "place" becomes just another concept in the university curriculum. Without the development of ecological literacy and critical understanding of the cultural and gendered constructions of place, a sense of place is no longer a force for ecological and social justice.

The best nature writing is invaluable in holding this tension. Eric Rolls' language comes out of long experience of the Pilliga and its inhabitants; it *informs* the reader about the bird and tree species and their surprising interrelationships; it *provokes* the reader to question received wisdom about the history of the Scrub, to wonder how human beings and animals can possibly cohabit; it *inspires* the reader to pay closer attention to his or her own place. While doing all of these things, it sings of the Pilliga and grieves for the destruction that is occurring, providing an example to the students of how to call forth an experience of the wild onto the page.

If work like this, and other fine examples from Australia and North America,[6] can evoke place experience as well as engender personal, ecological and political awareness, where is the tension? Partly it is in the timing of the educational process—students need to suspend all kinds of judgments about what they are doing, especially self-judgments, and immerse themselves in a place, trusting the process to see that there is a point to simply sitting quietly, listening, observing, sketching. This is in itself a radical act in a world in which everyone seems to be increasingly busy, and children and adults spend much of their day in front of a computer or television screen. Nature writing that celebrates such immersion and "attention of the heart" has an important part to play at this stage, yet critical awareness of the pitfalls and dangers of place attachment must also be brought to the fore.

There are "pathologies of place", such as place essentialism (considering that a place has a fixed identity or character—"the real Manly"), parochialism (excessive attachment to one place at the expense of other places—gentrifying one suburb while diverting all the traffic into another) and neglecting different cultural and gendered understandings of a place (the cities that some male nature writers revile may be places of liberation from traditional male authority for women). Such matters have led critics such as Doreen Massey[7] and George Seddon[8] to ask "Whose sense of place are we talking about?" Furthermore, it's all very well to inform, provoke and inspire individuals to greater awareness of place, but if we live in a society whose political and economic institutions systematically act to deny and thwart nourishing place relationships, what's the point?[9] If Australia is full of expressions of love of the land in prose, poetry, music and film, but there are ongoing assaults on soil water, plants and the worst rate of mammal extinctions of any continent, then what kind of love is that?

I tend to take a developmental approach to such questions. Expressions of love of country can start as fairly naïve sentiments, but can be worked with by paying attention to particular places and developing the capacity for felt response that is more likely to lead to practical action. As individual and community action becomes more place-oriented, governments respond to some degree (witness what has happened with Landcare), and there is the possibility of slow evolutionary change (from the "bottom up") in our political and economic institutions. If these changes are truly going to lead to ecological and social justice, it is very important that students are exposed to the critics of place attachment, to become aware that even such an apparently benign phenomenon as a sense of place can be problematic, and to adopt a critically reflective stance towards their own place affiliation and its origins.

Hence, my set of readings includes a section of critiques of the place-attachment literature as well as a section of nature writing. I don't ask nature writing to do all the work of a place educator, nor should it. However, to the extent that the nature writer is aware of his or her construction of a sense of place based on the perspective of a particular culture, class and gender, and reflects upon the need for sustained action by people who have become more sensitised to place, he or she will be assisting the work of place-based education rather than unwittingly contributing to injustices, or worse, perpetuating pathologies of place.

To return to the Faulconbridge country in which I started this essay, I have begun to wonder just how much my teaching and writing has been influenced by the place itself. Woodhouse and Knapp[10] note that a distinctive characteristic of place-based education is that "it emerges from the particular attributes of a place. The content is specific to the geography, ecology, politics and other dynamics of that place". It is clear how the *content* of my teaching draws on the particularities of the Blue Mountains. When I stand, looking across at the massive sandstone bluffs with a group of students, it's easy to see the geological story of sedimentation and uplift writ large. I can take them through the consequences of deep vertical jointing and erosion to nutrient poor soils, specialised vegetation and the consequences for animal life and subsequent human habitation.

There are also more subtle effects on the *process* of place education than Woodhouse and Knapp allow for. There is a large sandstone overhang in the upper mountains under which my students roll out their sleeping bags on soft beds of tree fern fronds next to a small cascade into a deep rock pool. They are physically and psychologically held and supported in such a place, allowing me to draw them deeper into sensory and affective exploration than if we were in the jutting slate country to the south that has no such declivities. Upon reflection, I can see that in response, I have emphasised those aspects of place education that are in sympathy with such an environment— containment, nurturance and healing. I do not claim a causal relationship, as if my teaching is simply a product of the physical place, but an interactive effect of my deepening participation with the places in which I live and teach. My writing has also been an integral aspect of the participation, as a means to reflect upon experiences that might otherwise be taken for granted, to communicate them to students and other writers, and to help create the conditions in which place-oriented community action is fostered.

I have a growing sense of participation in a process much larger than myself, a network of complexly interdependent relationships of place, narrative, self and other that take me deeper into this sandstone country I inhabit. Within this network, my evolving place-based education practices and my place writing are both outcomes of place relationship and contributing forces for its further development. I suspect that the "person-sized" hollows and overhangs, and the life that they shelter, still have much to teach me.

Notes

1   J. Cameron, "Dwelling in place, dwelling on earth" in J. Cameron, ed., *Changing places: Re-imagining Australia* (Sydney: Longueville Press, 2003).

2   Vicki King, "Embodied Perceptions: Body and Ground in Aboriginal Expressions of Place" in J. Cameron, ed., *Changing places: Re-imagining Australia* (Sydney: Longueville Press, 2003).

3   H. Bortoft, *The Wholeness of Nature: Goethe's Way Towards a Science of Conscious Participation in Nature* (New York: Lindisfarne Press, 1996).

4   Eric Rolls, *A Million Wild Acres* (Melbourne: Penguin, 1984).

5   J. Cameron, "Educating for place responsiveness: an Australian perspective on ethical practice", *Ethics, Place and Environment*, 6.2 (2003) 99–116.

6   see also Mark Tredinnick, ed., *A Place on Earth* (Sydney: University of NSW Press, 2003); J. Woodhouse and C. Knapp, *Place-Based Curriculum and Instruction: Outdoor and Environmental Education Approaches* (Charleston, West Virginia: ERIC Clearinghouse on Rural Education and Small Schools, Charleston, 2000).

7   D. Massey, Space, *Place and Gender* (Cambridge: Polity Press, 1994).

8   G. Seddon, *Landprints: Reflections on Place and Landscape*, (Cambridge: Cambridge University Press, 1997).

9   V. Plumwood, "Belonging, Naming and Decolonisation", *Ecopolitics: Thought and Action*, 1.1 (2000) 90–106.

10 J. Woodhouse and C. Knapp, *Place-Based Curriculum and Instruction: Outdoor and Environmental Education Approaches* (Charleston, West Virginia: ERIC Clearinghouse on Rural Education and Small Schools, 2000).

ROBERT ADAMSON

THE YELLOW CHINESE PARROT

Water colour moon, fogged up window panes.
The river, out there, slips by
as a branch from a slanting blackbutt
inscribes the surface with a sparkling line.
Living near the mudflats, I'm
protected by mangroves—
in winter the southerly winds,
rake through their curly heads
and the green skirts are my windbreak.
My summer thoughts
are silted up with mud and all thought
becomes obscure. All I have
left are a few quips to offer the critics
of my swamp, even though
the young artists painting back new wings
are the true menace. Who cares now,
more than half way into a big ebb:
mud exposed is a dark moat,
if you get this far—watch it—
step on my dreams you'll discover
they've been pulped. It's only flight
that matters here, so take a break and fling your
next thought into the tide.
In these parts the yellow parrot must
carry its own cage on its back through the swamp.
You know, I once believed
these things, however this morning the bird
suffered a stroke, it's owner kept saying "It keeps falling
to the ground, nothing can be done". Time
to commiserate with this bird, all colour but not quite parrot.

THE GREENSHANK

for Juno

In a trench, Miklos Radnoti
noticed it was spring, petals of crushed flowers
floated in a wake of scent.
His lover's face appeared, he caressed her neck,
then wrote a sonnet in his notebook—
lead flying, he scrawled words
with the stub of his pencil—

Just after dawn today, the news echoed lies.
Radnoti's love poem was wiped away
with wings and petals. Hungarian fascists
following their orders.

The full light, outside the windows,
your unbending will—
Our sanctuary, Mondrian's concepts
made of glass and cedar, this river chapel house.

This afternoon just before dark
the first greenshank from the Hebrides arrived.

Migrating across human borders
landing on the mud-bank.
It's technology feathers and fish-fuel, cryptic colours.

This elegant wader from Scotland's lowlands
ruffled in the westerly, took off again
and with an acrobatic twist skimmed over a hummock.

It's beak conducted the rising and falling of its song.
This lone greenshank dashed across mudflats
stood on one leg, then came forward in a high stepping dance.

EASTER: 2004 FOR JUNO & LUCY
    At Mooney Creek, my wife and her mother
    cook meals each night in the bright void
    of our kitchen.

    They talk of tough meals
    from another world, a brutal place at the other end
    that existed before new Jerusalem,
    the baked potatoes, the tart green bean soup.

    The top of a sunken mountain—
    through glass, curved lines of bush charcoal
    darkened as the sun dropped behind the world
    on Good Friday as we spoke
    of the Passover.

    Our conversation, spent words
    still humming, the shape of a butcher bird,
    started fluting its capricious scales—

    This music opened up my head
    and I drifted out, circled the room,
    wanting to fly across the darkening bays into an elegant
        apartment
    in Budapest to feel what drives people out

    Our minds can sometimes flower
    like monstrous kelp, waving in tide pouring
    from an old wound—

    We talked carefully, dinking tea
    soothing doubt. Tide pushed over
    the marbled surface of Mooney Creek—up stream, a pair of
        sea-eagles

    circled down to their nest.
    Sunset filled our heads with streaks of silent pain and the calm
    before the void, that impossible measure.

    We steamed and ate the mulloway.
    In dream you stood at the stern of the boat, our wake little
        cold flames
    of phosphorous lapping behind us, burning the words.

CUTTING THINGS OUT

I turned out the lights
and pulled the telephone out of the wall
saw stars through the cedar slats
I wrapped a scarf around my headache
and looked into a dark pit.

Nothing again, an ebbing memory—

I had to leave with the tide, the boat
roared to life and I hurtled across the river
into the blazing cold sunlight.

Now crouched in a dark corner,
my Siamese cat borrows my voice.
I speak to him, counting my dark blessings
the heater clicks, its pilot light blinks.

My thoughts embellishing the new untold lies.

THE VOYAGE

We looked up at Scorpio's tail of stars
curved across light years of night.
We anchored and made love in the dark.

We embraced in the cold before dawn
and spoke of Novalis who praised nocturnal light.
Although my thoughts were dark,

you said there were those who spoke of light
as they moved through the night:
old saints and fishermen following stars.

The river flowed towards morning in the dark.
Scorpio grew pale, fading into dawn.
If this is darkness, we sail into the light.

JOHN HUGHES

WHAT REMAINS

When I see such things, I'm no longer sure
that what's important
is more important than what's not.
    Wislawa Szymborska

I

I'm looking at a drawing. There's no way an artist could have made this drawing. A child, maybe, but I don't think so, for even in a child's scribble there is style. You could make a copy of it, that would be easy enough, but there's no way you could draw it, *ex nihilo*, out of your own head. It's got nothing to do with technique, or experience—Dürer would have drawn it five hundred years ago if it was only that. A trick, then? But there's no sleight-of-hand here—quite the opposite in fact. The drawing is beautifully simple; it wears its heart on its sleeve. And that is the key. No human hand could have made this drawing because no hand, however innocent, can escape the fetters of its style. The drawing is there, yes, it has been drawn, yet whichever way you look at it the question remains: who (or should that be what?) held the pencil? I'm looking at a drawing that doesn't have a style.

The style of the hand is as the voice which holds the song, as singular and unbiddable as the lace of a fingerprint. And yet this drawing asks us to allow the existence of a song without a voice. Or rather, Babel in one voice. There is no style here because there are hundreds of styles here. The artist who made this drawing had a hundred hands, each attached to a different mind, or no mind at all. Which, where style is concerned, amounts to the same thing. Lines left on a page with no eyesight colouring the hand.

Thin lines, thick lines, clean lines, broken lines, tight lines, loose lines, heavy, light, and feathered lines, dotted lines, smudged lines, bold and faded lines, curves and whorls and arabesques, spearheads, smoke wisps, whipcracks, sprayed, splayed, oblique lines, layers and contours and milky ways, worm lines, hook lines, cuneiform, runes and hieroglyphs, ideograms, alphabets and elusive symbols, endless alphabets—each the trace of death and the pressure of its touch, trace lines of the carbonised world, burnt offerings, skeletons, charcoal hymns, traces of fire.

John Wolseley

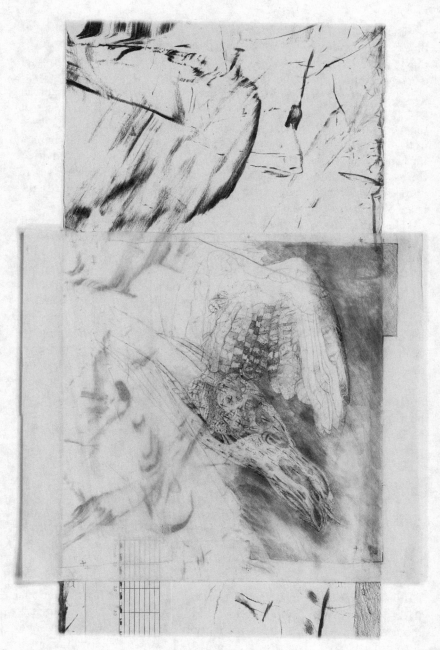

John Wolseley

45

The drawing I'm looking at was made by dragging a large piece of Blue Lake hand-made watercolour paper (made from reconstituted rags) against the charred remains of allocasuarinas, petrophiles, isopogon, dipterocarps, burnt mallee scrub and gahnia sedge. The trees didn't quite draw themselves, but in their dance with the heavy cotton paper they left the imprint of their carbonised forms, skeletal traces of their brush against the page. There is something of the Miró or the Klee in this—playful, delicate teasing, almost figurative forms (a kite there, a bird, a bottle, a moth, a snail)—but Klee and Miró contrived their forms, in every line there is eyesight colouring the hand, whereas here nature plays on the page, or, to be more precise, the page records the trace of the artist's play with nature.

The artist allowed the trees to draw themselves—he was their medium, but not their translator. The distinction is crucial here. To quote Wittgenstein: "If a lion could speak we couldn't understand it." In this drawing nature speaks, the lines of carbonised wood are its voice. But it speaks only because the artist has found a way to shed his own voice, to give up, not only his style but his very self—to become, in effect, no more than a living Ouija board. The word "living", like the distinction made above, is crucial. The trees that made this drawing are dead, the black skeletons of trees—it is the artist's motion that gives them voice—it is, strictly speaking, the dance that speaks, this waltz of paper and ash. The artist does not give himself up in advance; he does not and cannot empty himself by a conscious act of will. It is the process that frees him and allows the landscape, if only for a moment, to become that self that it has freed. In that instant when the two worlds touch, each for a moment becomes the other. We can't speak of collaboration here, for how can the stone, the ash (whose language is a shadow), collaborate? We must speak only of pressure; of touch.

When Ch'ui the draftsman, in one of the stories of Chuang Tzu, is asked how he is able to draw more perfect circles freehand than with a compass, how his fingers can bring forth spontaneous forms from nowhere, he replies: "When the shoe fits the foot is forgotten."

II

Late one afternoon, high in the Curra Moors of the Royal National Park, John Wolseley had an accident. He had been in the park for two months, drawn by fire and a fascination for what remained. A landscape of charcoal. The fire had purged all leaf, litter and blossom to leave skeletal trees of pure carbon; leaves, buds, bark pared down to the bare idea of Banksia or isopogon. Wolseley began to see in the blackness of these skeletal shapes some kind of graphic diagram of the essential nature of each tree. He was drawing these shapes next to cladograms (the Family Tree of a species as it has evolved from its origins) of each tree and marvelling at the strange resemblance, at how each carbonised plant form and its physical appearance in space seemed to mimic the cladogram form, the shape of its evolution in time, when the accident happened. The wind was picking up and shaking his easel so violently he could hardly draw. Then the large piece of paper and its support crashed over on top of the Isopogon he had been drawing. And somehow had continued drawing. For there, punctuating the surface of the paper, he saw the most rhythmic and lyrical charcoal notations. The thin black fingers of the plant, like some extraordinary drawing instrument, had left lines and marks of a kind he could not, intentionally, have drawn himself. He clipped a new piece of paper to the board and in a kind of dance moved the board against the burnt bush that surrounded him. He stopped and looked down at what could only be described as a record of the dance: each charcoal branch had registered its touch on the page, its sliding syncopated movement across it. Each charcoal branch had left its trace.

III

> If you persist in trying to attain what is never attained; if you persist in making effort to obtain what effort cannot get; if you persist in reasoning about what cannot be understood—you will be destroyed by the very thing you seek.
> Chuang Tzu

There is, in all visual art, something of the tension between distance and proximity. Two weeks after the fire, off the old Princes Highway, John Wolseley found a cave. He bought a tarpaulin and poles and an esky. He became for a time like the hermit of the moors. He would draw during the day and return each night to this cave cut beneath the burnt ground on which he had just walked, as if he had stepped through the looking glass into this emptied mirror image of the world above, the entrails of the land. He lived on bread, sardines, and milky tea. There was nothing self-conscious in this (it's the way he works), nothing of the vain and precious striving to become one with the landscape he wanted to draw; he dwelled within it, literally, he inhabited it and became, over time, not its coeval, but rather its trace;

its ghost. The work he finally produced, the landscape's dark imprint, might therefore be understood in terms of how the spirit might conceive of the body (the spirit's longing for the body)—if such a conception were imaginable.

But chance, too, must have its part. No matter how much he might try to narrow the gap between his physical experience of this strange carbonised world and the images he wanted on the paper (to breach that seemingly inviolable barrier between self and nature), the desire itself for closeness was always going to keep him at a distance. Even as he inhabited the place and allowed it to inhabit him, to sit and to draw kept him outside, beyond the elusive grasp of something essential. He wanted something more kinaesthetic, a more somatic method that would represent not what he saw (for what is seeing, if not a touch from afar?), but the meeting point of his impact with it. The solution came by accident, though accident is not, perhaps, the best way to describe it, as what could be more kinaesthetic than the wind? The toppling of the easel was more like an answer, an echo of the artist's intuition—his instinct and his need. The discovery was thus aleatoric, dependent on the throw of a die, a conspiracy of wind and paper, but what followed was not. The random quality of the marks on the page had something of the aleatoric beauty of John Cage's later work, a feeling of being some kind of musical notation, and it was this apprehension of a connection between drawing and music that opened the possibility for the harnessing of chance, a method of haptic mark-making.

Haptic, but not random. There is an element of chance in the way the marks land on the paper, but the method of moving whole sheets of paper over and around and through each plant (as if the paper itself has become the brush), seems to embody in another sense the Taoist idea that nothing is accidental. Each plant punctuates the air in the branching mode peculiar to its species and together they are like the trace of the land—a history of wind, rain and fire. Then the artist moves in with his drawing board, moves through the heath with a certain stride and rhythm, in tune now, and the scrape and dot and dance of it are there, caught like music, like a map on the page. The moment of each imprint an impossible alchemy in which the border between the artist and his subject dissolves; or, to be more precise, a moment in which, as far as the artist and the landscape are concerned, it is no longer clear who is drawing whom.

A variation. A 12 foot length of 300 gsm Saunders' paper, cut from a 5 foot by 30 foot roll, trapped at each end with 2 by 1 strips of pine, nailed together. Two artists now, one at either end, the paper held tight like a sail against the wind, pure white, a giant litmus ready to register the tiniest powdering in the air or the heavy impact of burnt black tree trunks. Moving down a ravine the length of paper becomes a variable line, tautening snake-like in its weave between burnt saplings. Arabesques of tiny charcoal lines, stippled shadows, traces at once frozen and fluid in the charcoal fingers' drag and flick and release. The hillside folds in on itself—hint of a pathway. Different kinds of encounter—hairy needle bush, hakea gibbosa, pink tea tree, native grasses, a giant banksia whose knobbled bark leaves a passage of black scales, a fossilised reptile scratching its rough back in magical animation. The artists move in interplays of rhythm, the paper sawing back and forth. Yet the carbonised trees are not passive. They move as if encountering wind, responding in a mix of pressure and release. The narrative of a journey, subtle changes from tree to sapling to scrub, traces of a natural progression, a strange kinetic map of a watershed going down into a valley, a map with no key other than the nature of its lines: the caress of slender petropile saplings; blunt anvil butts of the carbonised stumps of dead trees. One would have to have a mind of charcoal, really, to read such a map, to see how it had made of time itself a space. Memory is such a map, but a map that cannot be drawn; not like this. Perhaps, when the two artists stopped at the base of the watershed, the blackened valley opening before them, and looked, finally, at what had been drawn, they saw, even more than being within the land itself, that they were within the page and not just its observer; that the landscape, in drawing itself, drew them as well, a drawing together into some wonderful hybrid organism whose mind is fire.

Later, the artist in his studio. He is alone again. The 12 foot piece of heavy paper is tacked to a wall and he is drawing on it. Some of the marks are suggestive to him—sooty smudges like moth wings, feathers or flying seeds; insect jaw, bird shadow. Should he add to them now; continue the process that began when a smaller page fell on the burnt ground? When does the collaboration cease, or rather, can the collaboration set in train by his haptic method ever cease? Is there anything less aleatoric about what is done after? For the viewer, who looks after and draws in his own mind what he sees, there is no difference.

IV

What makes a drawing interesting? Our first instinct is to respond to all art as representational. We think the artist must be representing something and so the puzzle, the pleasure, is to work it out. For this reason, even in the most abstract works, we find (make) figures. The analogical mode of thinking is perhaps instinctual here, a semblance of the thing-making (or naming) we do all the time in language (that art is a kind of sign language, a representation of the relationship we have with actual physical forms). The delight, then, in finding (making) resemblances—the discovery of a trace of ourselves in all that we see; the power of bestowing, or remembering, a name.

Or is representation a barking up the wrong tree, here, and what we should really be considering is narrative; our need for story? At one extreme we have the genre of the narrative painting, the most explicit statement of this need. But at the other end of the spectrum, when confronted with the desperation of pure abstraction, the idea that the image tells us the story of its process of creation. As far as the narrative impulse goes, all art can be placed somewhere between these two extremes.

But do we look at landscape itself in the same way? Is our interest in nature defined by the same analogical processes of resemblance and narrative (dried-out riverbeds like drawings in the earth, for instance, fossilised traces), a mirror image of our response to art? What is the landscape, then; what do we mean when we say this word? If, in what we are looking, we are already finding traces of what we have seen, making resemblances, in what, might we say, does the difference between looking at a landscape and a representation of a landscape consist? John Wolseley, in his bush fire drawings, addresses this question in perhaps the only way it can be addressed—analogically: the difference between looking at a landscape and the representation of a landscape is the difference between wood and ash.

A good translation is a fire that leaves, like ash in the new language, a trace of the original. A good translation creates a kind of language, a style that has not existed until that moment and could not be created *ab ovum* by a writer writing in his own native tongue. Every word in a good translation is like an echo, a shadow that is also, somehow, the light that throws it. John Wolseley's bush fire drawings can be seen, in this sense, as translations, not only in terms of the language they create, but also, and more importantly, because of the consanguinity they suggest between translation and representation. The larger pieces actually look like the landscape and a map of the landscape; we know they can't be both (a map can't be the space it represents), and yet, like the new language created by a good translation, they are. There are moments, when you look at these works, that you feel as if they are the reality and the landscape their flawed representation. The trees and burnt-out bushes are but signs to the landscape hanging on the wall. It's as if you're looking at the contours of the moor, the trees and shrubs and land itself, yet you know that somehow you are also looking at uneven, wandering, uncontrolled, styless charcoal lines. And it is this very stylessness that is the magic here: the landscape made by fire, the object of the artist's gaze, is the very landscape made on the page by what remains, the object of the charcoal's graze: the sublime stylessness of fire.

V

> Even the wind
> Leaves its shadow
> On the dunes.
> Her footprints
> Like an echo in sand.

John Wolseley's bush fire drawings extend what has been a lifelong meditation on ways of imaging land by taking us to the heart of the idea of image itself and its difference from the trace; between the image of something as formulated in certain conventions of drawing and painting (the inherited system of conventions and signs, a symbolic accretion that grows like crust on the eyes), and those various signs and markings which are the traces of what was once there: abrasions, stains, negatives, watermarks, fossil imprints, rock pool whorls, footprints, ash, smoke and refuse—what remains.

At a spot in the moors where twigs and branches had collapsed on the ground and lay like layers of bought charcoal in a box, the artist came across a dead, half-burnt wallaby. Feeding on it was a mass of blowflies and a huge goanna, ripping the thighs. Death keeping the lizard alive and birds fluttering over the lizard's head catching flies. A ripple under the skin of maggots. An endless metamorphosis as one kind of living thing transformed into another.

None of this creation would have been possible, of course, without fire, without the burning, and hence carbonisation of wood. Landscapes cannot ordinarily draw themselves. Living trees leave no trace. Like the great and terrible goddess Kali, who, at the end of each cycle of universal destruction, garners the seeds for the next creation and preserves them like an old peasant in her own "hotchpotch" pot, destruction and creation are magically one. The charcoal traces are like the voice of this metamorphosis, a primal speech which emerges like life out of death, from the blackening of wood. The voice of which I speak is not the artist's voice, the figure in the landscape sitting and sketching an image of burnt trees; the voice of which I speak is of the trees imprinting themselves on the page, this final act of creation only possible because they have been destroyed by fire—traces of the departing spirit. Like the word (itself the trace of thought), gone with the breath that carries it.

And do those traces, like a negative, speak of a body disappeared, or a body just waiting to develop?

Charcoal is the trace of wood, and it carries within itself the trace of "coal", the carbonised matter from which and to which it comes. The tactile nature of so many of these drawings, diagrammatic equivalents of pelt and fur. Seducing the hand, as if touch alone can make them complete. Charcoal is the spirit of wood; nature imprints its remains. Touch the page and it passes to the hand, the imprint, spirit of the tree. Dirty, the beautiful dirtiness of them. Why children love playing in mud, presenting their excrement in proud offering to their parents—pure delight in what remains. The trace of the hand on walls and clothes and skin. We lose it, don't we? don't like it at all now; we shudder a little, fear a little, for the clean white shirt, painted wall—black world/white world—colourless all-colour—traces of what we leave behind, are and are no longer. Wood, or the spirit of wood?

The child's first marks are scribble. Insects leave the shadow of their motion in the dirt. Eucalypts weep in resinous scribble. Babbled drawing. The origin of the image in the trace. Origin of the word, scribbled in the throat.

A detail where the trace suggests a shape that resembles a thing— an insect, in this case, as if the plant contained within itself the idea of the animate world it would draw in. Terrible word that, suggest— membrane, boundary, border, skin; name by which all forms remain discrete and name by which they collapse into one. Here, the work of the eye, or the artist, later in his studio. Protean impalpability, infinite mutability. A bird? A moth? Membrane between trace and thing; membrane between trace and eye. A footprint is clearly an image of a foot, a figurative trace, we might say. But what is ash, or a shell, or these black powder prints of burnt sedge? Images still, but of what? I can't get the idea of language out of my brain. It flickers like a shadow behind all I've written here, unseen, just off the page. Bird prints in sand, rock pool whorls, tidal stains—cuneiform, hieroglyph, ideogram. What remains of a conversation? Only the words. The voice leaves no trace, lest it shape the ear as an ammonite shapes its fossil shell, or wear the lips as the wind wears line into rock—the trace of air. Cuts, scars, bruises—language, too, of a harder voice also jealous to be heard.

Written language begins in the trace, the magic of what remains. In this sense every word, every character in fact, is essentially ideogrammatic in its claim to stand for the thing. Even the Roman script in which I make these words carries, like memory, the scar of this trace, the echo of its magic. The words themselves are like the child's wonder of words when first he senses their connection to things and the way this connection is already a transformation, something magical: that the words in his mouth, and later, that the words on the page, are connected somehow to the world beyond himself, the world beyond the page; but also that these words, when connected, become something else. And that the magic goes further: that he can swap these words, these tiny fragments, for the world outside and be perfectly happy with the exchange; that nothing is what it seems. In this sense the ideogram (the word) is like a trace of what it represents—a trace, not an image.

A gesture; an analogy—something standing for something else.... It might be the first sentence. Two shaggy men watching an eagle circle, then stop, then drop as if through a trapdoor in the air. They don't see the hare until the great bird, at the still point of its drop, snatches the small creature in. Terror-numb, heavy as a child, it doesn't kick or flinch, drawn upwards like the carriage of these wings and gone. The larger of the men has paused and seems to think—an absence in the way he holds his spear. Before him, on the plain, bison graze, and taking the smaller man by the arm he points at the bison and then at the eagle with his spear. There is something here of the origin of words—not that they stand for things, if that is the order, rather the other way around: that the thing might stand for the word.

Dreams leave their trace; memory, too, is a stain.

In his essay "Cinders", Jacques Derrida writes: "What a difference between ash and smoke: smoke seems to lose itself, and better, without leaving a sensory residue, but rises, takes the air, becomes subtle and sublimates itself. Ash falls, weary, heavy…" It's no accident, then, that smoke has come to stand for that which is ungraspable, the transitoriness of life, the spirit itself, whereas poor ash is what has been left behind, the mortal residue. Soul/Body. I wonder, though, about this distinction. Perhaps John Wolseley's bush drawings point to some other truth: the leaden ash, dragged and impressed upon the page, looks exactly like smoke, or more hauntingly, the fire from which both came.

VI

trace (treis), v. Forms: 4 trais(e, 4-7 trase, 4-trace. [ME. Trace-n, a. OF tracier, 12th c. (trasser, traser, traicier, etc), F. trace-r = Sp. trazar, It. tracciare to follow by foot, to trace, indicating a pop.L. or Com. Romanic tractiare, f. L. tractus a drawing, dragging, trailing, crawling; a train, track, course. The primary meaning of the verb was app. 'to proceed in a line, course, or track'. The early sense-development in OF. and ME. is not very clear, and some of the senses attach themselves immediately to TRACE sb. in its sense of "mark left by anything moving, footprint", itself a derivative of the vb. in its earlier senses.]

I. 1. *intr*. To take one's course, make one's way; to proceed, pass, go, travel, tread.
2. *intr*. To pace or step in dancing; to tread a measure; to dance
3. *trans*. To pass along or over, tread (a path, way, street, etc.).
4. *trans*. To travel or range over; to go or pass about, around, or through; to tread, traverse.

II. 5. a. To follow the footprints or traces of; esp. to track by the footprints; also with the traces as object; hence, to pursue, to dog.
b. *fig*. To follow, pursue (instructions, example, etc).
6. *fig*. To follow the course, development, or history of. Also with the course, etc. as object. b. intr. for pass. To trace its origin or history; to go back in time, to date back.
7. a. *trans*. To make out and follow (with the eye or mind) the course or line of; to ascertain (the course or line of something).
b. To make out (worn or obscure writing); to discern, decipher.
c. To make a tracing of (a listed item); to derive (a tracing) from an index or catalogue.
8. a. To discover, find out, or ascertain by investigation; to find out step by step; to search out.
b. To discover evidence of the existence or occurrence of; to find traces of.

III. **9.** *trans.* To mark, make marks upon; esp. to mark or ornament with lines, figures, or characters: cf. TRACERY.

10. To make a plan, diagram, or chart of (something existing or to be constructed); to mark out the course of (a road, etc.) on, or by means of, a plan or map; to mark or set out (the lines of a work or road) on the ground itself. Also fig. to devise (a plan of action), map out (a policy).

11. a. To draw; to draw an outline or figure of; also, to put down in writing, to pen.

b. To copy (a drawing, plan, etc.) by following the lines of the original drawing on a transparent sheet placed upon it; to make a tracing of.

Note

The sections dealing with John Wolseley's methods are based on his own account published as "Bushfire Journals" in HEAT 4. New Series: Burnt Ground.

ROBERT GRAY

JOAN EARDLEY IN CATTERLINE

The black-faced sheep
are titled in the storm-light and they face the black-faced
North Sea
on the long decline

of the swollen
pastures. Across all of this, a similar
inertia. The weeds and fence posts come down and hang
above the lane

and we pass underneath
the banks that ooze like a luminous, wrung-out kitchen cloth.
    A barn
opens on a corner
its tunnel

directly out of the gravel
kerb; we slide
by in a car, swishing over mashed cow manure and sliding
    water.
Joan Eardley

came here,
following the reports
on the news, to a place with the worst of
weather, to a cove

that in itself is rough as the jaws of a wrench.
The tight cottages
are fastened to each other and along the buckled headlands
of tight grass; one row on either. Otherwise, there is a pub.

She brought her cancer,
stepped down
into the rattling edges of the bay, with an easel
of lead pipes, it must have been. The storms here are like the
    water's turmoil

in a toilet bowl or
a furnace door
opened on wind and snow. She stood in the sea,
the water ahead higher than her painting board.

We saw this in Aberdeen's
quiet gallery. The sea fell like a weir,
corrugated in black and white. The sky was seasick, a
    greenish-grey; the grey sea
greasy as stone, and its foam

yellow, from the churned-up
shallow floor, or else
there was the release, the transformation, of peach blossom
on black sticks. She broke open

the paint, wound it together, squalled her graffiti
along the water's face, scoured
with blunt spines, tightened everything under a clunky
    spanner, swabbed,
undid through a slice of the trowel, dug

her fingernails in, engrossed. Her subject,
death's approach,
become subject
to her. It was painting as judo.

Or she turned inland, into the passages of the sun—
to an over-ripe
pecked fruit,
which at other times seemed a snivelling, dangled

mucous, and at times had the liquid redness
of an organ
squashed into a jar. The sun, among
the broken panes

of the sticks
and the long grassy skeins,
waning,
was also painted as her own,

with an urgency occluding distance and time. Bits of straw
   and rope
and grass seeds and bent nails were caught up,
among paint
that she lived in like the mud. Joan Eardley in Catterline at
   home.

I think of someone great,
of Dogen, in his death poem. "For fifty years I have hung
the sky with stars; and now I leap through.
What shattering!"

SCOTT SLOVIC

THERE'S SOMETHING ABOUT YOUR VOICE I CANNOT HEAR: ENVIRONMENTAL LITERATURE, PUBLIC POLICY AND ECOCRITICISM

"I'M SORRY, MS. WILLIAMS, there's something about your voice I cannot hear."

There's something about your voice I cannot hear. This was Utah congressman Jim Hanson speaking to nature writer Terry Tempest Williams after she had presented her essay "Bloodlines" as testimony during a public hearing in southern Utah regarding wilderness preservation in that part of the state in the mid-1990s. The idea that there are certain kinds of voices—certain modes of discourse—that are unheard, and perhaps unhearable, in public discussions of environmental values and policy is what inspired me to join up with Canadian anthropologist Terre Satterfield and begin working on the book titled *What's Nature Worth? Narrative Expressions of Environmental Values* seven years ago, a work finally published this year. The images and stories embedded in "nature writing," "environmental literature," or what is sometimes called "the literature of place" are now widely recognized as some of the most potent literary creations in recent years and throughout history. But what does such achievement mean if we are doomed to lose the places and species that have inspired such eloquence? What do any artistic and scholarly achievements mean if we are fated in the coming decades to see our own species contort itself to pass through what American environmental journalist Bill McKibben recently called "the ecological bottleneck"?

We must find a way, I believe, to help those toiling in the realms of politics, economics, law, and public policy move beyond the constraining discourse of those fields and appreciate the values-rich language of story and image. Colorado author and legal scholar Charles Wilkinson argued in his 1992 book, *The Eagle Bird: Mapping a New West*, that it is crucial to "change the language of the law in order to change the terms of debate" regarding species, habitat, and natural resources in the American West. He lamented that "legal language... is bloodless. It seems that attorneys are imbued with an absolute compulsion to wring every last drop of emotion, passion, love, and grief out of every single sentence" (10). Somehow, this professor of law maintains, we must find a way to deepen and enrich the language used by the public—and by public officials—when talking and writing about our relation to the natural world. He states:

> If the language among the people changes, the language in the law books will change. One task is to add new kinds of words to balance out a vocabulary now dominated by board feet and cost-benefit analyses. The other task is to enrich existing words. When we hear a forester comment that timber harvesting will 'sustain the productivity of the land,' we should ask, 'Productivity for voles?' When enough westerners understand that concept, law and policy will fall into line. (15–16)

The process of transforming our official legal, economic, and governmental language from that of bloodless contractual arrangements to empathetic stories that might enable us to imagine the issue of forest productivity from the perspective of a vole (a small, mouse-like mammal) will require monumental ambition and verbal acrobatics. This is, and has perhaps always been, the ultimate ambition of writers and critics exploring nature and culture, at least in the United States. Contemporary author Barry Lopez once famously remarked, "I suppose this is a conceit, but I believe this area of writing will not only one day produce a major and lasting body of American literature, but that it might also provide a foundation for the reorganization of American political thought" (297). Environmentally oriented literary scholars— known as "ecocritics"—have been tracking this transformative process in such works as Daniel G. Payne's *Voices in the Wilderness: American Nature Writing and Environmental Politics* (1996) and Daniel Philippon's *Conserving Words: How American Nature Writers Shaped the Environmental Movement* (2004). *What's Nature Worth* seeks to contribute in a different way, spurring the process of merging literary images and stories with the discourse of public policy by presenting interviews with twelve leading environmental writers about the connection between story and environmental values, providing brief samples of their work that illustrates this connection, and contextualizing each example in a framework that should be accessible to economics, lawyers, and policy specialists.

"Is language an ultimate answer?" asks Charles Wilkinson? "Not remotely. Is language a sound, constructive, and necessary beginning? Absolutely. In our society, often through law, we set the essential context for action through our official language. By that language, we invite inquiry by the human imagination or clamp imaginative inquiry off; we set a high tone or opt for business as usual" (19). Although many environmental writers and ecocritics prefer to work for social reform through the gradual, subtle media of traditional literary and scholarly publication, classroom instruction, and occasional public talks, others are opting for more direct approaches—writing to public officials, joining the boards of activist organizations, and preaching to audiences other than the choir.

* * *

Allow me to backtrack a bit and discuss two central facets of environmental literature: how this writing guides us to pay deeper attention to our physical senses and enables us to appreciate our own embeddedness in the world, and also how this writing enables us to develop and clarify and articulate our feelings about the world's meaning, its value.

I often find myself referring to Scott Russell Sanders's 1987 essay "Speaking a Word for Nature" (from his book Secrets of the Universe) as a key articulation of what literature needs to do if it's to get us to acknowledge the ecological implications of our presence on the planet. In this essay, he critiques the tendency in popular contemporary American writing, especially fiction, to ignore nonhuman nature. He calls such writing "pathological" for its avoidance of reality, its neglect of questions and issues crucial to the current and longtime survival of our species. Sanders writes:

> However accurately it reflects the surface of our times, [literature] that never looks beyond the human realm is profoundly false, and therefore pathological. No matter how urban our experience, no matter how oblivious we may be toward nature, we are nonethe-less animals, two-legged sacks of meat and blood and bone

dependent on the whole living planet for our survival. Our out-
breathings still flow through the pores of trees, our food still
grows in dirt, our bodies decay. Of course, we all nod our heads
in agreement. The gospel of ecology has become an *intellectual*
commonplace. But it is not yet an *emotional* one. For most of us,
most of the time, nature appears framed in a window or a video
screen or inside the borders of a photograph. We do not feel the
organic web passing through our guts, as it truly does. While our
theories of nature have become wiser, our experience of nature has
become shallower.... Thus, any writer who sees the world in ecological perspective faces a hard problem: how, despite the perfec-
tion of our technological boxes, to make us feel the ache and tug
of that organic web passing through us, how to situate the lives of
characters—and therefore of readers—in nature. (226)

As Sanders suggests, the great difficulty encountered by writers who
tend to be attuned to their personal experience of the world and the
implications of that experience is how to communicate their ideas to a
readership that, first, may be more interested in watching television or
film than in reading, and, second, has little direct experience of the
nonhuman world. I live in a fairly typical suburban neighborhood in
the United States, where large houses cover entire lots and the most
prominent features of many homes are the multiple garages for cars
(sometimes as many as four or five garages per house). I seldom see my
neighbors—they drive home from work, electronically open their
garages, and then close the garage doors by remote control after they
drive in. This is a metaphor for how they live their entire lives, more or
less, enclosed within human constructions. Compelling such people to
think of the ecological implications of their lives is an uphill challenge.
But it's a challenge that many contemporary writers and artists
nonetheless feel compelled to take on.

I believe we need literature—or art more generally—to help us use
our senses more fully and intensely. We need to overcome the
abstractness of our ecological awareness and learn to live through such
awareness, to feel our presence in the world. Writers in general—and I
find this particularly true of so-called environmental writers—serve as
extensions of our own nerve endings. They feel for us, they exhort us to
feel more intensely, more fully, and they demonstrate the processes of
sensation in a way that we can then enact more consciously.

"How sense-luscious the world is," writes essayist and poet Diane
Ackerman in the preface to *A Natural History of the Senses* (xv). How

many of us actually go through our lives thinking this, aware of how our senses are connecting us moment by moment to the rest of the world? It's the purpose of most if not all of the people we call environmental writers to do just that—to help us overcome the idea of ecological connectedness as an arid abstraction and to feel it as a vivid, visceral reality. Read Australian essayist Eric Rolls's *A Celebration of the Senses*, for instance, or Japanese-American farmer and nature writer David Mas Masumoto's 2003 book of nonfiction, *Four Seasons in Five Senses: Things Worth Savoring*. Read novelist James Dickey's 1970 classic, *Deliverance*, for an allegory of sensory awareness, showing how several characters overcome the ennui and alienation of their suburban lives by experiencing the vivid beauty—and the pain—of a direct encounter with wild nature.

Fiction is often a particularly good genre in which to present narratives that are readily perceived not only as specific stories but as allegories that mirror readers' experiences. There are many fine examples of environmental fiction that functions allegorically to demonstrate how engagement with the world through our senses might somehow revitalize us and enable us to live more conscious, meaningful lives. One fine example is David James Duncan's 1983 novel, *The River Why*, in which the narrator is a fishing prodigy who comes to learn that it is important for him not only to know *how* to catch fish, but to appreciate *why* he finds it useful and meaningful to have such interactions with fish, with nature. Another is Tim Winton's 2001 novel *Dirt Music*, in which the character Luther Fox "goes bush" and finds himself profoundly enmeshed in the reality of nature, realizing, "The world is holy? Maybe so. But it has teeth too. How often has he felt that bite in a slamming gust of wind" (361).

The idea that we can begin with personal sensory experience and then quickly build upon such experience in order to develop a better understanding of large-scale ecological processes is well explained in environmental education scholar Mitchell Thomashow's recent book *Bringing the Biosphere Home: Learning to Perceive Global Environmental Change* (2002). Thomashow suggests that we can use our senses to explore connections between our own specific places in the world and the rest of the planet. He argues that it's crucial, if we're to know what's happening in the world during this time of significant changes, for us to think in terms of relationship—particularly, the relationship between our place and other places, our moment in history and other times, past and future. Several of Thomashow's points specifically tie in with the role of literature in helping people to "bring the biosphere home," to understand the big picture of the "biosphere" (the planet and its atmosphere) by way of close attention to "home" (where we are at any given moment). Here is his explanation of the methods of his own practice of "biospheric perception":

> First, I emphasize the importance of routine experience. In the course of your daily affairs and adventures, you have all the material you need for interpreting global environmental change. Biospheric perception is a practice you can engage in wherever you may be. In the time and space between your busy tasks, you can take a few moments to reconsider where you are, have a look around, and notice the sky, the landscape, and other life forms. In just a few moments you can travel a considerable conceptual distance through the biosphere. Second, I accentuate the narrative experience. I probe the stories that emerge from childhood memories, travels, and conversations, in conjunction with imaginative forays. To perceive the biosphere requires comparing times and places, different views you've had of the same spot through many years, understanding how your perceptions change by presence or absence. Imagination and memory often work together to conjure impressions that you may not attain in any other way. Third, I encourage you to carefully observe what you observe—knowing your proclivities and interests, assessing your insights, figuring out your perceptual and ecological strengths and weaknesses, the things that you see as well as the gaps, and using good teachers to help you in this. Fourth, biospheric perception is a community practice, something you engage in with other people. It takes lots of folks pointing things out to each other to reap the deepest insights. Fifth, I emphasize the importance of global change science as a means to provide balance and ballast for your observations. The biosphere is not necessarily what you project it to be. It involves processes and patterns that are empirically derived.
>
> Finally, I wind through a shifting phenomenological and existential passage. By phenomenology I refer to the great insights that can be derived from one's direct sensory impressions. To practice biospheric perception you must aspire to probe the full potential of your sensory awareness. By existential I convey the impression that we are investigating ideas and concepts that we can never fully understand. (16–17)

All of these cognitive processes—attention to routine experience, articulation via story and image, exploration of memory and imagination, precisely focused sensory attention, engagement with other people, absorption of formal scientific theories and information, and the asking of deeper phenomenological and existential questions—characterize the standard elements, both subtle and overt, of so-called environmental writing, environmental literature.

* * *

So far I've been discussing how environmental writers guide readers to pay attention to the world. One of the crucial questions about literary accounts of such sensory experiences of nature is how they will affect readers and, further, how such writing might eventually have an impact on environment laws and policies and on the daily behaviour, even the conscious and unconscious world views, of other members of society.

Remember the passage with which I began this essay, the oft-quoted statement by Congressman Jim Hanson—it may someday be printed on his tombstone—"I'm sorry, Ms. Williams, but there is something about your voice I cannot hear." Comfortable with and accustomed to the discourse of law and economics, but less so with the language of story, at least in a public policy context, Hanson could not pick up the useable, values-related aspects of Williams's narrative—they somehow eluded his hearing, his comprehension. Here are the opening brief paragraphs of Williams's two-page statement:

> There is a woman who is a tailor. She lives in Green River, Utah, and makes her livelihood performing alterations, taking in a few inches here, letting out a few inches there, basting in hems, then finishing them with a feather stitch.
>
> While hiking alone in the San Rafael Swell, this woman was raped, thrown down face-first on the sand. She never saw the face of her assailant. What she knew was this: in that act of violence she lost her voice. She was unable to cry for help. He left her violated and raw. (Qtd. in Satterfield and Slovic, 80–81)

The woman responds to her experience by returning to the site of her attack and leaving symbolic "fetishes" here and there in the desert: "The woman cut pieces of thread and placed them delicately on the desert. Six inches. Three inches. Twelve inches. They appeared as a loose stitched seam upon the land." Eventually she approaches a particularly magical place that has been named "the birthing rock" by native people. Here,

> The woman picks up an obsidian chip that has been worked by ancient hands; the flaked edge is razor sharp. She holds it between her fingers like a pencil, opens her left hand and traces her own life-line from beginning to end. The crescent moon below her thumb turns red. She places her palm on the boulder and screams. (81)

This story has no simple, explicit message about environmental policy or wilderness preservation, but in its richly emotive and imaginative language it suggests that human life is deeply associated with specific places on the planet. The woman character, when attacked in a beloved landscape, must restore her attachment to that landscape by using thread and scissors—the tools of her craft—to stitch herself back into place. She has lost her voice, her sense of empowerment, in the initial attack, but when she guides the sharpened, pencil-like stone across her hand and imprints her blood upon the land, her voice, her scream, her sense of power and pain returns.

For the *What's Nature Worth?* project, Terre Satterfield and I conducted in-depth interviews with a dozen distinguished U.S. environmental writers, ranging from Native American authors such as Simon Ortiz and Ofelia Zepeda to former rancher William Kittredge and celebrated ethnobiologist Gary Paul Nabhan. It was our goal specifically to use these writers as "lay ethicists," as people who devote their lives to using language as a way of understanding the value of nature. We view such writers not as academic specialists in the field called "environmental ethics," but as storytellers who work every day to understand the value—the meaning, the importance—of their experiences in the world. We asked them questions about their approaches to writing stories, essays, and poems. We asked them to reflect on how information might be packaged within the medium of story. We asked them whether they wrote to convey their values to audiences or to explore, for themselves, the value of particular experiences or phenomena. We asked them to speculate about the broader social impact of narrative discourse that conveys a sense of environmental values.

In the lengthy introduction and the contextualizing essays at the beginning of each chapter, Terre Satterfield and I explain the current state of environmental values research in the United States and Canada and discuss how environmental law and policy tend to rely almost exclusively on economic processes for determining the value of natural phenomena (thinking of nature, for the most part, as a set of "resources" rather than as a realm of phenomena that may have value, or meaning, beyond human economic purposes). The primary method for determining the value of resources, particularly when certain kinds of degradation have occurred and compensation must be provided, is an economic tool known as "CV" (or contingent valuation), which involves the positing of a hypothetical market for whatever is being assessed—if you were going to purchase the Great Barrier Reef, for instance, how much would you pay for it? Put together a cluster of such evaluations, basically pulled from thin air, and, voila, there you have it: the value of the Great Barrier Reef. Our project emerges from a fundamental distrust of merely economic means of determining environmental values, our feeling—shared by many people in the arts and humanities and in the general public—that certain important facets of human values are getting left out of the economic processes, the economic equations. These aspects of our values systems cannot easily be reduced to numbers—to dollar amounts or ratings. Often the only way we can initially communicate such meanings, such values, is by telling stories that express our intuitive appreciation for certain places or phenomena.

In our interview with Terry Tempest Williams, the author suggested that the tension between the language of story and the language of law, economics, and policy is not necessarily a bad thing. She argued against neatly merging the various modes of expression. "I don't think you can manufacture or manipulate this connection," she said. "Stories arise out of the moment and that's where the power lies. You can't know what story is appropriate for any given moment. I mean the stories are born out of an organic necessity, out of the heat, and that is the source of their potency" (67–68). According to Williams—and perhaps Charles Wilkinson would agree—formal ideologies and mindless, inherited language start to break down when narrative language is introduced into policy discussions. Williams hopes, through her work, to help our culture "fall in love again with language and stillness and slowness," believing that this will enable us to make better, more sustainable decisions about how to live on the planet (69).

"I'm sorry, Ms. Williams, there's something about your voice I cannot hear." Despite the inability of one impatient politician to "hear" the message of a nature writer's story, this kind of language—narrative discourse, steeped in values born of specific landscapes, specific homes—plays a vital role in the lives of everyday people around the world. Laypeople, artists, and government officials, when asked what's really important to them, often turn to tales of experience and hope.

One of the crucial roles of ecocritical scholarship is to help make such tales audible in the halls of power.

Works Cited

Diane Ackerman, *A Natural History of the Senses* (New York: Random House, 1990).

James Dickey, *Deliverance* (1970. New York: Delta, 1994).

David James Duncan, *The River Why* (1983. New York: Bantam, 1984).

Barry Lopez, Contribution to "Natural History: An Annotated Booklist" *Antaeus* 57 (Autumn 1986: 295–97).

David Mas Masumoto, *Four Seasons in Five Senses: Things Worth Savoring* (New York: Norton, 2003).

Bill McKibben, "Global Warming, Genetic Engineering, and Other Questions of Human Scale" (Nevada Museum of Art, Reno. 12 March 2004).

Daniel G. Payne, *Voices in the Wilderness: American Nature Writing and Environmental Politics* (Hanover and London: UP of New England, 1996).

Daniel J. Philippon, *Conserving Words: How American Nature Writers Shaped the Environmental Movement* (Athens: U of Georgia Press, 2004).

Eric Rolls, *A Celebration of the Senses* (1984. Brisbane: University of Queensland Press, 1998).

Scott Russell Sanders, "Speaking a Word for Nature" *Secrets of the Universe: Scenes from the Journey Home* (Boston: Beacon, 1991).

Terre Satterfield and Scott Slovic, eds. *What's Nature Worth? Narrative Expressions of Environmental Values* (Salt Lake City: University of Utah Press, 2004).

Mitchell Thomashow, *Bringing the Biosphere Home: Learning to Perceive Global Environmental Change* (Cambridge, MA: MIT Press, 2002).

Charles Wilkinson, *The Eagle Bird: Mapping a New West* (New York: Pantheon, 1992).

Tim Winton, *Dirt Music* (Sydney: Picador/Pan Macmillan Australia, 2001).

CHRISTOPHER KELEN

TAI MO SHAN/ BIG HAT MOUNTAIN

1
every night the mountain climbs over

whatever I dream
it remains

beginning up
the mountain sits
for the world to roar round it

"Big Hat Mountain"—
when I get past the treeline
the sun will show me what I'm not wearing

these feet before me as elsewhere mine

great volumes of the sky halt here
that the lungs might touch what makes them

past last of shade of people sparse
I move mountainously

the track stands across my climbing

2
trees themselves climb
—making, losing breath like me
who bends them? who's bent to them?

everything calls me away...
look this leech!—a watch,
my fur grown into garments,
to hold the mountain off

head full of, eyes too, mouth full up
even in this making silence
I cast none of this off

paradox—this stillness sweats from me
my presence in my means deferred
that I belong where I'm no part
and have not hide nor nesting

I take the mountain up
now time has pitched its tent in me
the city's trafficking sloughs

enough blank space

3
smoulders into its autumn burden

someone is burning in the dry gully

...through the thickness of air
a broken umbrella caught in tree forks
the broken wind burnt here

far below tugs work the harbour dry
the sea faced off in its cargo of sunk truths
        its grim old forevers as good as today

4
a day with the mountain—what does it mean?

the wind is like rubble piled
in a silent forest where the birds
have lost sway

then the forest itself bends under divinity

centuries back the mountain gets into me
I must climb

the mountain can only be taken the wrong way:
shrines and incense fall up its sides

in the way of devotion

folk bring their birds to sing with the wild
the wind stirs up in its corners
as the sound the ear must stir from a shell
Big Hat—and the city like ears sticking out

faith occults the gradient
as if the mountain were to be believed

5
striding in the sun's vast strokes
my wrist minutely glints
I bring this cast of light on the mountain
to borrow an intensity

sun stands either side—can't be found out

I pull the mountain up over my head

bears my sullen breath away
the mountain confesses me
I have only to come

there is something between me and it
and not a form of understanding

to take up with the mountain
is the hardest thing to do

eyes down at my pencil
the mountain won't grudge
does not need to remember
has forgotten nothing

the boredom of the mountain
bigger than any of us

what is that speech below silence there?

6
breath down in rich seams older than speech

I am taking down the mountain's portrait
opinion of the place

in each lit square
faces pay for the privilege
of turning their backs on the mountain

a fine roof for all that has buried and built
and the sun singing down there
past roots, past all dim hoards
lost before measuring ever began
all that the mountain is
a fine roof

7
this going nowhere stills my bones
the better of me got

as home yearns for me
how could it not

when I myself am pacing elsewhere
how should the mountain manifest?
who can see it in me?

morning slouches with the mountain
noontide stands over, sun takes a set, quickens,
sky of bones and insects forgetting

a mountain of words against the mountain
symptom of which is self-erasure

climbing the mountain
I am invisible
does this get me nowhere?

stones washed raw
the mountain in theory is indivisible
if it leaves by the truckload
truckloads are left

8
some divination senses me

under these weathered hands of season
I make out the character for mountain

a bell sounds where the path comes still
which deities does the mountain guard?

faces worn with kindness uphill

in shanty sides and tricks of dwelling
even this bent old joke of a mountain
half erased and ready for more
eyed but if the dollar bids
idle in such fraught desire
I honour hoping that there's honour in it

9
uphill choose one rock
to sit on the mountain
limbs rest
two bodies together

which stills the way?

the fewer my footfalls
the more in the mountain

stood among clouds
its windows thin mists

my mountain on the window here
of which the clouds are capable

10
dusk is a last turn wrestles the mountain

descending, picking burrs from clothes
plucking ants from my fur
sweat dries cold
chill sets on my neck
I learn I have given the mountain my scarf
further down the mountain offers a glove
and then another for the same hand
different, another colour
I decline again

look in the morning
—how the mountain still stands
no hint of gloating

11
still life that we have ornamented
catch the angles from
it casts over
pales by
comes under a spell

nights home
I face the mountain
my building casts a shadow over
the mountain shows no face
I play the guitar a tune on the mountain

quavers like sparks spun
the stars—such comrades dim about me

the mountain frames
days buried
looks on in its auspicious graves
inauspicious though to look

once in a hermitfold black night of barking
under your smoky blanket of breath
grass curls up toes
jackhammer blowtorch—these are the fauna

a postcard in the museum of what was the mountain
a foolish old man grinds tiger bones

12
after the day's tides lock up the mountain
we all do, on all sides
the mountain is no longer at large

ever since night upended here
these bells wrung in this vindication
the mountain pursues me in my darkness
and in my knots of future

I kneel for the mountain until it recalls me
—we have all the world's time here

god of the mountain answer me this
to be true to this place and to the earth under
to be true to this air, my here and now
whom must I mock? how?

MARGARET SOMMERVILLE

TO COOLOOLA[1]

STRETCHED OUT IN A CURVE

Cooloola Campaign I: In 1953 Kathleen and Judith stood on top of Mt Tinbeerwah and looked down on Cooloola, "spread out in a curve right into the ocean, a wonderful stretch of sand full of trees with water on both sides, no road, no nothing, it was so beautiful".

The Cooloola Campaign began in 1953 when Kathleen McArthur[2] and Judith Wright stood on top of Mt Tinbeerwah and looked down on Cooloola, and ended in 1975 when it was officially declared a National Park. As we talk in Kathleen's living room now, she gives me an image of Cooloola as woman, "spread out in a curve right into the ocean". Voluptuous, excessive, lying on her side, curves and folds of sensuous body exposed. When she talks about Cooloola now, in her 82nd year, she becomes young, almost girlish, and she says "I cannot give you the stories of Cooloola". When I ask her how I can know Cooloola, she tells me I must go there. So I arrange to go to Cooloola with Kris Plowman, ecologist, conservationist, heir of Kathleen's work, and her stories.

I have come to Midyim to spend a day or two with Kathleen before we go. It is midday and Kathleen and I are sitting in the little gathered-together warmth of winter sun at the fish and chips shop at Kings Beach, Caloundra. I ask her which bits of Cooloola she likes best, "all of it" she says, and I think yes it is a whole, a body of sand. And I ask her what is so special about Cooloola. "The high dunes" she says, "it is the only place where the dunes are so high that they hold water in aquifers which is released when it rains to form creeks and lakes, river and rainforest. It is the diversity of it all." A body of sand: sea, beach, dunes; rainforest, wallum, swamp; lake, creeks and river.

We look at a letter that has just arrived from Judith. In it Judith remembers the wildflower plains of Cooloola and the house at Boreen Point which she bought after she and Kathleen had seen Cooloola from Mt Tinbeerwah: "I remember so many lovely wildflower stretches that must now all be gone. I only hope that Boreen still has some; and I remember (do you) the name of Melaleuca written in Jack's best handwriting on the cottage wall, and hope that too survives" (Letter, Judith to Kathleen, 30/7/97). We talk about their friendship now, the stories that intertwine them inevitably with that place. Kathleen says that it was in the cottage at Boreen Point that Judith had uncontrollable bleeding and had to go to hospital for a curette because she was pregnant. In this conversation I am initiated into a privileged world of women's knowledge. It is about caring, and the loving that moved outwards from Judith's and Kathleen's friendship into that body of sand. Kathleen and Judith made many trips to Cooloola, up the Noosa River. "I hope you see the fruit bats", she says, "the night flowers that attract them are a bit later, but there might be something. It's a wonderful place, Cooloola. Boreen Point would be a good place to stop first if you can make it there, but it is tricky getting out of the lake. How far you get will depend on the tide and the river".

INITIATION

Cooloola Campaign II: After seeing the sandmass from Mt Tinbeerwah, Kathleen and Judith went to Boreen Point on Lake Cootharaba to find a way in to Cooloola. They went on a tour to the Upper Noosa River, walking through the bush to Lake Cooloola and another tour across Lake Cootharaba and down the Teewah Track to Laguna Bay Beach to see the coloured sands. They fell in love with Cooloola.

That night in Boreen Point, on the edge of Lake Cootharaba, dreams are intensified. Loud rain pelts on tin roof, and sleep is ragged with raging rivers and angry rising lakes. Demons rise and fall with rain on roof, higher peaks stirring up terrors of boats on water, from years of living on an island with babies, rough waves, little row boat. There are no roads in and no roads out—only the boat. And haunted by the lines of Judith's Cooloola poem, "the invaders feet will tangle/in nets there and his blood thinned by fears". Judith says we live in a haunted country, torn between our love of the land and the guilt of invasion.[3]

What if I am not supposed to go into this country?

In the early morning Cootharaba is squally wind-whipped waves and pelting rain blowing horizontally across the wide open space of the lake which grows larger by the minute. I want to abandon ship before I get in, retreat to the safety of the motel room, read about Cooloola instead of doing it. Only the thought of Kathleen, and the quizzical look of the young boat-hire man, makes me hide terror and pack things into the hull of the little outboard, trousers rolled knee deep into the cold rainy day. There's a quick lesson on how to drive—"start with a bit of choke and a bit of accelerator, gears are forward, neutral and reverse on the handle, always start in neutral, pull the throttle and off you go". He pushes us out towards the middle of the lake, 'you go out through the markers for about 25 metres, and then head towards the sand patch'. Scudding into waves and wind, we turn right towards the sand patch. It is soon too far to swim in any direction. Teresa de Lauretis says our femaleness clings to us "like a wet silk dress".[4] To drive this boat across Lake Cootharaba is a battle against this clinging sense of physical inadequacy. But then there is a lot a girl can do with a silk dress. As women we move into the landscape differently. We knit together different sorts of compromises, with no desire for conquest.

Time is suspended in the middle of the lake. Squally wind and rain blows in gusts, soft rain is quiet and peaceful, but halfway across the wind whips up a storm. Panic rises in pit of belly, boat engine is drowned by roar of wind, and I think it has died or run out of petrol. Sand patch disappears and the whole world is grey wetness with no visibility in any direction. By concentrating hard on the place where the sand patch was, I can see the faint outline of two curves on line of horizon, just above the sand patch. Breast curves stay on skyline even when all else disappears. After forever we find a red marker, and navigate our way through guide buoys to the quiet water of Kinaba Rangers Station on the other side of the lake. Climb out with wet clothes clinging and hair dripping in channels down face and back to pay our dues to National Parks—but even they're not home. Cootharaba has initiated us.

ENTER THROUGH THE RIVER

Cooloola Campaign III: After their initial visit to Cooloola, Kathleen and Judith decided that the beautiful wallum country of wildflowers and the sandmass with its system of river and lakes would make a unique National Park. They wrote to Romeo Lahey of the National Parks Association and he responded that it was not threatened in any way, whereas there were important areas of rainforest that were, and his association gave priority to those. But the mineral sands prospectors had already arrived in Cooloola.

Beyond Cootharaba lies another world. Wind and rain gone, winding between tiny islands and narrow channels, river appearing and disappearing. There are pelicans on sandbanks, brown ducks and black swans on the water and cormorants on logs drying their wings. Around the bend into the everglades, quiet stillness of sinuous river, brown silk, winds its narrow passageway through a magic world. Fine pink hair tufts of reeds, broad green leaves of swamp banksia, and tattered flesh-coloured paperbark, flank the water's edge, at times almost meeting overhead. All is reflected in smooth brown silk of river's surface until it is impossible to tell where bank ends and reflection begins.

To know Cooloola, and to represent it, that is the challenge. In coming to know Cooloola I think about the landscape as subject, an active being that reaches out to me. As Kathleen says, it is what the landscape gives me. My body is the register of sensations of smell, touch, light, colour, warmth, movement and taste. It is also the act of representation that shapes landscape words—trying to write the immediacy of it. "The body and not only the ear, is a trembling flame, a vibrating surface, ruffled water. The body does not photograph the world but filters it across permeable membranes"[5]. My skin is the permeable membrane upon which Cooloola is inscribed.

Through gusty winds of Cootharaba, deep stillness of the narrows and puffs of light breeze on skin as river opens out, I come to know the shapes of this place. With air on skin comes the smells of the river, salty over Cootharaba, fetid smell of decomposition as river closes in and lighter river smell as it opens up again. Through movement of body, buffeted across lake and quietly snaking around bends of river I know it as if I was without sight. To look at the river is to touch its silky surface, as tannin soaked smoothness crinkles ever so slightly with reflections of all around it. Through the river we enter Cooloola.

CAMP

Cooloola Campaign IV; The idea for the action came in the form of a postcard that had been used successfully in the United States. Kathleen immediately took up the idea with the Caloundra branch of the Wildlife Society and the words of protest were printed on the back of the postcard. "Your Government's failure to declare the whole of Cooloola a National Park, in the face of mounting public pressure is deplorable. The only acceptable use for this unique wilderness is its immediate dedication as a National Park".[6] On the front was the address of the Queensland Premier, J. Bjelke Peterson, Parliament House, Brisbane.

It is a camp of trees, shady filtered light. On one side of the entrance, a tall white scribbly gum glows and on the other, the stocky strength of an old and twisted wallum banksia guards the way in. At eye level it is only trunks, skin of trees, soon recognisable skin against skin. Deeply grooved grey of casuarina, round nodules of gnarled Banksia aemula, and huge smooth fleshed angophera with hollows and folds of her own. We sweep away leaves, twigs and nuts to make a clear patch of soft grey sand to lie on and pitch our tents. As we boil a billy sitting in the firelight, Kris tells me Cooloola is about learning to grow old in the landscape.

Australia is like a geriatric person, tough, unforgiving and fragile. An aged landscape must always be treated with veneration and respect. It is a tough old lady like Kath, clear about its ways of doing things, clear about how it wants to do it, tough and so beautiful. The younger stuff is by the sea. Right on the coast there are very steep sand hills, almost cliff-like, dropping down to the sea with brush box and Banksia aemula, one foot tall, fully formed trees. Then in the mid dunes there's open woodland because there has been time for organic matter to build up—blackbutt, brushbox and sometimes rainforest trees, figs and palms. Further west, the older dunes go into scribbly gum and Banksia aemula. It is poorer soil again; they are smaller, sparser, not as much wood. So what you're seeing as you walk across the Cooloola landscape is a living succession. It is living with the landscape's birth, maturity and ageing, and then they die sometimes. This is amazing to see in microcosm, to walk across it, from now to 400,000 years ago in a day. It is outside of time.

At night we live by sound. First the sound of our storytelling, then the sounds the landscape brings to us. Rain pit-pattering or louder drumming, drowning at times the distant roar of the sea and croaking frogs on the nearby plain. I listen to all these water noises, pattering or drumming of rain, rhythmical hum of distant sea, frogs on wet plain and imagine, very close, the silent, sinuous movement of the nearby river. Our sleep is also punctuated by the sounds of night visitors. Scrabbling of little native rats on my tent, and something else making a loud clattering of dishes and food bins. Just before dawn I am glad to hear the "cheep cheep" of the Eastern yellow robin, the first bird call before a crescendo of bird song rises to challenge the patter of the rain.

Out in the wet camp an empty sardine can and olives have disappeared and Kris says our oil-loving night thief is a dingo.

CEREMONIAL

Cooloola Campaign V: An information brochure was written to accompany the postcards describing Cooloola as "a triangular island complex of wild flower heaths, giant dunes, rainforests, fresh water lakes and the Teewah coloured sands. COOLOOLA MUST BE SAVED, and the Queensland Government, instead of encouraging proposals leading to the destruction of its unique landscape, should be far sighted enough to condemn such unnecessary exploitation".

The afternoon is bright blue with puffs of cloud as we walk to the sand patch. The soft white sand track, pressed and dimpled by rain, winds through wallum country of low Banksia aemula and bright wildflowers. There are pink boronia, yellow pea flowers and purple irises—silken skirts wet with rain. On top of the ridge we wander along the dune, in and out of open forest, and we soon glimpse the light of the sand patch through grey-green foliage and dark trunks. This brightness comes and goes until suddenly we come across the fullness of it. Around a bend, up a short incline, trees end and the whole huge body of sand sprawls naked over the top of the dune reflecting whatever light is in the grey and foreboding sky. Surface of sand is smooth over curves and undulations but close up it is dimpled by rain, like pore marks on skin. Across the middle, a single track of dingo.

The sand patch tips off the edge where the distant blue of water merges into the grey blue sky. Below us Cooloola is stretched out like a map. On this side of the blue haze, the eye can just make out huge Cootharaba, long narrow form of Lake Como, skinny river winding in and out and Lake Cooloola round and fat in the foreground. Like the series of internal organs linked by the bloodstream river on Kath's mud map of Cooloola.

The sand patch is fringed by bushes that it threatens to engulf as it moves backwards and forwards across the high dune. We slip into this fringe of leaves and eat lunch in its leaf litter hollow on the edge of the sand. Around us we find ancient pipi shells and stone tools uncovered by the continual movement of sand. Like all of Cooloola, the sand patch is inhabited—by dingo, by us and by all the people who walk to the sand patch because it is a special place. It is inscribed by stories of inhabitation, past and present and I wonder why we all go to the sand patch. Why does dingo go there every day? Why are there ancient pipi shells and stone artefacts there? And why do we, and many others, make the pilgrimage up to the sand patch today?

I think that it is not inhabited as dwelling place but as a ritual, a special place. It opens out a great stretch of Cooloola to lay at our feet. It has the particular Taoist qualities of stability as a marker while also being constantly mobile. One side of the sand patch is surrounded by skeletons of dead trees from the most recent shifting of sand. It is somehow shocking in the strength of its living, embodied quality. Even the archaeologist, in a dry scientific report, comments on its trailing arms and sprawling mass. It has a special energy that is at the same time sacred and profane. And as Kris says, if you disturbed an area at the top of the high dunes enough you would make another sand blow. Perhaps it was made by people coming to the top of the high dune to see all that you could see below it, thus creating this special place.

Capillaries of water

Cooloola Campaign V: 100,000 cards, 10,000 brochures and letters were ordered and, while these were being printed, Kathleen established an address list of the names of every organisation in Australia that was in any way connected with the environment. This included scientific societies, natural history and bushwalkers clubs, tree societies, wildflower clubs, shooters associations, forestry and garden clubs and many more. Each of these was sent the letter, brochure and five postcards. From then on, Kathleen writes, "the Premier was getting a big mail. The letters, telegrams, phone calls and personal calls left no doubt that the Cooloola postcard campaign had touched a national nerve"[7].

That night the pitter patter of rain continues but somehow, during the night, I give up my desperation for dry weather and become resigned to getting to know this world of water—a baptism by water. The rain is soft and I sleep in the soft heartbeat of its sound. During the night I begin to bleed and wonder about managing with only four sanitary pads in this water wet world. I creep out of tent into the curved hollow of a nearby angophera and leave two clots of deep red blood shining in the wetness. I cover them with leaves and in the morning the leaves are moved aside; blood gone, dingo visit.

Morning wash in the river is quiet and still, mirror smooth surface dimpled by concentric circles of occasional raindrops. Wash with care—no soap, detergent, shampoo in river. I take off my clothes and soap myself a little way up the bank with half a billy of warm water from the fire, sloosh off the soap then slip into the bottomless brown silk of the river. Tea-coloured water envelopes skin of arms, and my body glides towards the finger reflections of paperbark, satin water sliding over bare skin.

Dry sands form some of the most barren places on earth, and it is water in the sands of Cooloola that give it life. In this water wet world I imagine water as circulating like blood through the body of Cooloola linking its organs, giving it life. I remember Kathleen saying before we left that "the dunes are so high, they hold water in aquifers which is released when it rains to form creeks and lakes, river, rainforest". The textures of this country are made by water and you can read the presence of water in the landscape. When you walk across the landscape you can see where the water is. Down by the river you know how wet it is because that is where the water loving roburs and paperbarks are growing. The little pink reedy swamps are sloshy and sinkable and the big swamp breathes and glows its swampy airless decomposition into the darkness of night.

The dry sandy wallum plains need water to begin life, and to sustain life there. In the Cooloola wallum country, rain is part of an infinite network of waterways, filtering through the body of sand, making life possible.

VISCERAL KNOWING

Cooloola Campaign VI: 6000 postcards were returned. The issue was debated in Parliament and the media. Many letters were received in response to the campaign, "We do sympathise with your cause and trust that those in high places can be made to realise their responsibilities to coming generations. J. S., Launceston, Tasmania". But the Government replied that it had always been their policy to protect the coloured sands and they had no intention of declaring it a National Park.

By mid-afternoon it is clear again as we walk on the track that skirts the river on a narrow platform of high ground between the river and the low wet plain. As we walk there are pockets of different places— with different plants, smell, quality of light, life forms. The feel of the place changes. We catch the strong aromatic smell of a lilli pilli tree, drawn to its purple fruity perfume. We eat a handful of the shiny purple fruits with crunchy white flesh and mild tart taste. How would we survive if we had to live off this land?

From the weirdly layered trunk of the grass tree we collect resinous splinters to light a fire in the wet. We pick a handful of half dry tea tree twigs, drier than anything on the ground, and drag them along behind us making scrawls on sandy track. On a high spot of silver sand we sit for a while to eat a mandarin and watch the ants as they dance around our discarded mandarin pips. There are two sorts of ants who dance approach and retreat as they meet each other and then one lot goes off and leaves the others to the sweet delicacy. Kris says there are over three hundred species of ants in Cooloola, which rivals quite diverse rainforest environments. We wander along, going nowhere in particular, stopping to look and see, exploring and collecting, learning to be in the place and we begin to ask

How do we inhabit this place and how does it inhabit us?

We learn to live in Cooloola in a "visceral" way, responding to what it gives us. We find the soft sand to lie on under the sheer membrane of our tents at night. We work out how far our bodies will stretch out into Cooloola in one day and then again the next and the next; where to find the bits and pieces that will light a fire in the wet; where the dry places will be to walk and sit; and where to hang our clothes to get the slightest breeze for drying. We learn the tracks in and out of the camp and who comes on them to visit us at night. We learn to find food from trees and bushes around the camp. We stretch out into Cooloola with our bellies.

In Cooloola there is a whole mosaic of vegetation depending on where on the sand mass you are. If you are down by the river, as the water runs off the dunes down to flat area, you go from aemula and scribbly gum where it is dry to robur and swampy things, lemon scented tea tree and ghania where it is wet. That is a very broad description but within it there are pockets of this and pockets of that, depending on where water might gather, what the aspect is, whether there are hollows and bumps, how close the water table is, how old the sand is. What has happened over time since the sand was deposited. Who has lived there before—who can live there afterwards? How well they've lived affects who comes later and how they, in turn, can express their form. These are the mosaics of place.

REPRESENTATION

Cooloola Campaign VII: The campaign for Cooloola saved the Noosa Plain but many thousands of hectares of wallum flowers were destroyed in the 1970s with a scheme to create improved pastures for cattle. Then there was to be a hearing in the Mining Warden's Court of the Mining Application in early 1970. To keep Cooloola in the headlines over the Christmas period and then on into the months leading up to the Mining Warden's hearing, Kathleen wrote articles in the local paper on Cooloola wilderness gardens and others on the Noosa River with "photographed reflections that spoke louder than words". She painted a collection of wallum flowers as a greeting card, naming it "Cooloola Wildflowers".

Knowing Cooloola cannot be separated from our representations of it. Kris's stories are the stories of an ecologist with a sense of wonder and connection. Even though you can know something in its factual scientific detail, the mystery of putting it all together makes a complexity that is greater than the sum of its parts. There is also the intimacy with which you can know individual detail and the stories of unlikely aspects of the natural world that are not usually included in popular discourses of conservation. It is easy to love a koala bear but much more difficult to persuade people to care for ants. Kris is an ant specialist and tells stories of "the sisters" because "ants are all female and live in co-operative colonies in the ground". She tells me the story of the leptomyrmex ants that we watched eating juice from our mandarin pips.

Kathleen represented Cooloola in her wildflower painting. Her painting of "Cooloola wildflowers" glows in between the pages of my notebook. It was painted to impress people with the beauty of the sandy wallum country of Cooloola. Dancing coloured silk of bright pink nunniyum, purples iris, deep golden guinea flower, paler soft gold of native hibiscus and the pink fringes of pigface. It is in the texture of petals that Kathleen's representation is so seductive. Beautiful coloured skirts show crinkles and veins, folds and feel of skin surface of these flowers. And there is the shock that a harsh and spare environment like Cooloola can produce such gaudy colours and textures.

Every day, sometimes several times a day, I write from my body as the "ruffled surface" that registers all that I can see, smell, touch, taste and feel of Cooloola. Through that writing I come to know Cooloola more intimately. The discipline of making the separation from immersion in place to the writing of it, the effort of the symbolic, sharpens the powers of perception, makes the senses more acute. But what of drawing, I wonder. How does Kathleen's perception, mediated through her painting of wildflowers, change what she knows about her places?

Late in the last afternoon of our final day at Cooloola, it is clear enough to go down to the river and draw the little patch of trees and scrub that guards the entrance to our camp. I want to know what it means to engage with a place in this way; to learn the art of seeing by making that connection from landscape to eye and hand to paper. I draw single leaves at first, slender serrated leaf of Banksia aemula with long central vein and single three-stemmed fern, tiny opposing leaf couplets each side of three wiry stems growing smaller and smaller until finest fern frond curl at tip. But then, how to put all these things together, how to convey the feel of the whole of this little patch of bush—Cooloola mosaic in miniature.

I see a wild and chaotic messiness of shape and form, each crossing and intertwining the other so that it is often unclear which bit belongs to what. On the ground a froth of fine green ferns rises up, more air than matter, defined by the spaces they make. Rising from this froth, strappy ghania leaves are bent over and heavy brown seed heads rise up from their centre. A new grass tree begins somewhere with a shower of leaves spilling out from the centre and out of this seems to emerge big and small trunks and branches of trees constructing the space with their flesh. As the light fades, the patterns of their shapes give way to quiet sounds of the river.

IMMERSION

Cooloola Campaign VIII: In the news of 3 March 1970 they learnt that objections to the mining application must be in the Gympie Mining Warden's Court by 20 March and would probably be heard in May or June. Now was the time to seek donations towards the cost of the hearing. So Kathleen went back through the files and letters, looking for those who had responded to the postcard campaign and sent out a circular appealing for funds. The appeal was responded to with such generosity that the sympathy and concern was obvious. Every donor deserved and got a handwritten letter of thanks.

At nightfall we sit by the river's edge, with a drop of rum and a slice of sweet halva and watch the quiet darkness of the river. Even the sound of a tiny creature scuffling in and out of the reeds rustles our quiet contemplation. This last night we decide to row on the river just as darkness falls. We row until a blush of pale apricot lights dark the outline of trees to the west. Then we drift on the surface of water as the last light fades, moving only with the slightest current of water and eddy of air. Reflections of the day gone, the river dons its night-time finery of black silk and silver. A silver quarter moon and evening star appear in dark sky above, echoed in black silk below.

That night, in my tent, all is still and silent. She is so quiet tonight,

Cooloola, this body of sand. Sea almost indiscernible breath, lovers whisper. I think of you Cooloola, smooth round curves of abundant woman and am small, smaller than an ant and move intimately over the surface of your skin. I trace the line of flesh from broad sweep of shoulder over curve of breast, hollow of underarm, mound of belly, crevice of groin, long line of strong leg. Linger over curves of sand patch, long slow curves and hollows bordered by fringe of dark bushes, surface dimpled with finest pores, skin of breast. Shelter in hollow, silky fringe of hair and over mound of belly, buried in soft flesh, crinkles of palest purple satin inlaid into pearl, marks of skin running towards the river.

I think of the river through which we come to you Cooloola. Silky brown river winding in and out of narrow channels where sinuous brown silk reflects fluff of pink reeds and curls of fine finger-line of paperbark skin until it is impossible to tell where outside ends and inside begins. Night-time slip into silky blackness, river of desire, rippling over skin, stroking softly as it closes over my body and across my breast there is diamond star and crescent moon on black silk. And inside organs of Cootharaba Como Cooloola Coroiba, wrapping tongue around Kabi tongue-clicking names, body organ shapes of lakes joined by sinuous network of lines of blood. Cooloola's river, oh Cooloola.

RETREAT

Cooloola Campaign IX: The great day came in August when the Joint Parliamentary Parties decided there was to be no mining anywhere in Cooloola. Four years later in 1974 the Cooloola National Park was gazetted.

In the morning a white mist hovers over the silent river but, as I watch, the mist clears and pink-edged clouds appear in perfect reflection in the river's upside down world. Our camp is drip-dripping as we pack tents and the sky clears to light grey and then blue as we move down the river in reverse order of our coming: ast huge gnarled old trees, eucalypts and angopheras and deep rainforest, with glow of cabbage tree palm and tall palms reaching out to the sky; past Harry's hut and the place where Judith and Kathleen's sock marked the track to Lake Cooloola; past the narrows where pink hair tufts of reeds and broad leafed ghania are perfectly reflected in the brown silk river below; past the channels and tiny islands, pelicans, ducks, swans and cormorants and into the big open space of Lake Cootharaba. Cootharaba is clear blue and choppy, flickery wind blowing this way and that whipping up little flickers of anxiety. Then the boat glides in to the sand and we stop for a while in the quiet stillness of Boreen Point. Getting used to people and different pace after the intensity of Cooloola.

At Midyim Kathleen is waiting for us. She waves from the front window in her whiteness. She has everything ready, the postcard from the Cooloola campaign, addressed to "The honourable J. Bjelke Petersen", "Your Government's failure to declare the whole of Cooloola a National Park, in the face of mounting public pressure is deplorable. The only acceptable use for this unique wilderness is its immediate dedication as a National Park". The leaflet that went out with the postcard "Why Cooloola?" On the back, the now familiar map where I trace the tracks of our journey and tell Kathleen our stories of her beloved Cooloola.

> body of sand
> spread out in a curve
> right into the ocean
> full of trees
> water on both sides
> a dreaming
> Cooloola
> after coolooli,
> Kabi name
> for dune cypress

Notes

1   This writing is a condensed and adapted version of 'Body of Sand' from *Wildflowering: the life and places of Kathleen McArthur* (Brisbane: University of Queensland Press, 2004).

2   Kathleen McArthur and Judith Wright founded the Wildlife Preservation Society of Queensland in 1952 and campaigned together for the preservation of many places, including Cooloola National Park in southern Queensland and the Great Barrier Reef.

3   Wright, 1991.

4   Teresa de Lauretis, *Technologies of Gender: Essays on Theory, Film and Fiction* (London: Macmillan, 1987) 12.

5   Paul Carter, *The Sound in Between: Voice, Space, Performance* (Sydney: University of NSW Press and New Endeavour Press, 1992) 129.

6   Kathleen McArthur, *Living on the Coast* (Sydney: Kangaroo Press, n.d.) 53.

7   McArthur, 53.

PETER HAY

POEM BY A LAKE

Suddenly a rinsed rag of sand,
a log in water with woolly tea-tree
rooting forth, their blind-gene reach of life
circumscribed in hard random luck.

Little poppering water sounds
finger my ears with love;
I thought: there is more power in water
than anyone can know.

A child's sky is pasted up with fluff
and, beyond the lake, unbreached there,
the forest's cross-stitched mantle,
its great intricate quickening.

And beyond that, on the next ridge,
or the next, or the next,
are the chains and the biting blades
that prove an animal clever, and blind.

SHEOAKS

The sea is grey, with the cross-hatched
back of an old man's hand.
The eyes that drop across it
have the vantage of a rock among sheoaks.

There are many rocks.
They are the bones of a time
when the penal station worked its farm here.

Sheoaks are dull and eldritch women,
knobble-skirted,
their small sloughed snakes a choke of carpet
on blighted ground.

Clouds come in on a wester.
The sea stirs with trapped mice.

The back upon the rock,
the back without eyes facing the trees,
the back insists upon a tigersnake's
terrible, purposeful approach.

The eyes and the back on the rock are perverse
and will not move.

The rocks are bones in the forest
and other bones are also here.
Small busy skulls with tenacious feather-tufts
are strayed penguins. Those
without feathers are pademelon.
Those others, forester kangaroo
urged namelessly here to add their bones.

The eyes hide a fear.
They regard the rock.

On the rock is the vigour of lichen,
grey, crust-yellow, rust.
But lichen is the much-wronged bloom of health
and the eyes take this for a good sign.

Now the wind comes in and the trees keen.
The land can hold no more sadness.
This is as pure, as concentrate, as it can be.

The back blindly regards the keening forest
and the death-bringing snake
and the old man's hand.

These are the crossing places.
Much might happen here.
Here the wanderers come, and unresolved things.

The snake is flat-eyed, deliberate.
The hand curls to claw.

In the forest that the eyes do not see
the forms may be black and quick,
brief candles of smoky sorrow.

In the forest that the eyes do not see
the forms may be raw abominations
wrung from the mad depths of the excoriated soul,
distilled here, chained and flogged and sodomized,
now foaming forth
just as the reluctant sons, the timid daughters,
have ever feared they would.

The sheoaks wait. They have time beaten.

With a controlled flick
and a nano-second's scaly coruscation
the snake is its length closer.

A back with eyes on a rock.
The eyes face the apathetic sea,
the back the worm-girdled women of the forest,
their silence and their keening song,
their bones,
the harboured grief and the hate.

The forest is a palimpsest.
It frames a fracture in time.

A scarlet robin
darts amid the carpet's gnarled worms.
The redbreast is life
and it dances past the eyes.

The eyes move and the back moves.
No snake. No old man claw.

Beyond the sheoaks is short, browsed grass
and the shit of living animals
and the little gold suns of the guinea flower.

PETER MINTER

THE SIGN AS NATURE STRUCK AT THE CAPITAL'S HEART

    Ozone seeps
       sand into air
inaudible at the studio mike's
    light penumbra
       under a stage tent

    curled pearl translucent
     in the gold grass   &

      wider out
our Capital's suburban lassitude
   sets hard around a lake's
      gelatinous weight

terrified sheep
    graze under vapour trails
      all across the Monaro

As you sing of Victor Jara
     in a cumulate hollow
morning arrests

    I see a young girl arrange grass
      clippings
runners and a rosemary stem
   in a careful arc on the stage step

      her pink powder blue Barbie cap
at eye level
    not hearing the song but
      holding its sense here—

to dwell on this planet,
   make shape.

     Of course it's just
a small arc, as we are

your hand wishing
    coiled notes from steel, or how
the earth I'm lying on
    knows the form of me already

    remembers
all the dead, our gentle

    bones' curve
        into the circling earth.

KATE RIGBY

RETURNING TO ROCKY NOB: STRAY THOUGHTS ON CANBERRA

There is a place where I like to stray in Canberra. I grew up thinking it was called "Rocky Nob", but I have since learnt that to most people that names the higher ground on the other side of La Perouse St. I went there rarely as a child. Mostly, my friends and I preferred the gentler terrain down near Flinders Way, with its soft grass, weeping willows and tiny creek that emerged into the sunlight for a brief stretch from the alluringly cavernous depths of a drainage pipe. Once, though, when I was about ten, I found myself alone on Rocky Nob.

A couple of years previously I had returned from a homesick spell in England to discover that the Canberra of well-groomed gardens, well-watered playing fields and well-fed children had acquired a certain unreality for me. It was as if the lawns and pavements to which I had hitherto entrusted my step were hovering a few inches above the ground, protecting me from a harsher truth, lurking beneath the surface of the comfortable middle class world where I had enjoyed such a happy childhood. That day on Rocky Nob, though, that familiar world suddenly disappeared from view, leaving me in a strange land, all sharp with long dry grasses, and brittle with the chitter of grasshoppers leaping about my legs with every footfall along the gravelly path, sending ants scurrying in all directions; a place, hot and hard as sunlight on stone, where, I suddenly recalled with a shudder, my father had once killed a snake (or so I believed at the time). A breach had formed in the false floor of Canberra, and I had somehow fallen to earth.

Yet there was also an intimation of something else in the shimmering atmosphere: a trace, perhaps, of the absent ones; those, black and

94

white, for whom this place, which for me was wild, was yet a world. I longed to linger, to enter more deeply into this hidden world. But fear overcame me, and I turned and fled.

In some ways, that flight, a flight from the wonder and woundedness of a homeland that was, and was not, my own, has continued until quite recently. I left Canberra as soon as I finished school, and the path of my later travels, studies and professional life led me far away from Rocky Nob into the heady world of European literature, philosophy and cultural landscapes. Only recently have I returned to the trail that I found, and lost, myself on all those years ago. My research on culture and environment in the Canberra region is still in its infancy, but already I am beginning to read Rocky Nob in new ways.[1] Those weathered rocks I have learnt to name Mt Painter porphyry, and to discern in them a story of ancient upheavals of the earth's crust, followed by eons of erosion, evidence of the more-than-human making of the land—and of the fragility of the soil.[2] Low in nutrients though it might be now, this soil nurtured the evolutionary emergence of a rich diversity of plant and animal life, which in turn came to sustain the vibrant human culture that grew up here over the millennia, altering the pre-existing environment, while nonetheless maintaining a high degree of biodiversity. I now know that descendents of the original Kamberri, the people who gave my hometown its name, still camped out near here less than fifty years before I was born. I had been given the impression that the indigenous people of this area had long since "died out"; but as recently as the late 1980s, Betty Homer could still recall visiting her uncle Roddy Williams' camp on Red Hill in the 1920s.[3] This year, on Easter Sunday, I had the privilege of joining with members of "Brindabella Dreaming," a Ngunnawal dance group, to stomp to the beat of a didgeridoo played by another of Roddy's descendents, Daniel Williams, amidst the regenerating bushland of the fire-ravaged Tidbinbilla National Park.

That day at Tidbinbilla, as well as celebrating the revival of Ngunnawal country and culture, I was delighted to talk with Eddy Green in what used to be his potato patch, looking across to the now sadly burnt-out house that his great grandparents built after they selected land there in the 19th century. On Rocky Nob, too, I can now discern a trace of the old pastoral landscape. In place of the succulent purplish-green kangaroo grass, carefully maintained by Aboriginal burning, which fed the first sheep and cattle to graze on the Limestone

Plains, tinder-dry wild oat predominates, and although yellow buttons and bluebells abound, I cannot spot any more tuberous lilies here now. Still, there are a couple of magnificent old apple box trees, and some younger red gums, as well as a few other species of eucalypt and several straggly acacias. Many of these trees, such as the invasive Cootamundra wattle, are not locally indigenous and betray evidence of the zeal for tree-planting that accompanied the creation of the federal capital. That is true also of the oak grove that I noted had grown up around one of the most striking rock formations back in the mid-1980s: self-seeded, I suspect, with the help of the cockies. I am a little saddened that this oak-grove, which once concealed a neo-pagan place of worship, has recently been felled, having fallen victim to the new zeal for purifying such places of the non-indigenous. On the other side of the rise, though, you can still find shelter from the sun and even a seat beneath the leafy fruit and nut trees that bear witness to an earlier impulse to claim a portion of this 'open' public land as a commons.

As I become more aware of the historical layering and cultural tensions evident in this one small corner of Canberra, I am led to reflect on some of the ambiguities that characterise the cultural landscape of the federal capital as a whole. Perhaps to a greater extent than any other city in the world, the built environment of Canberra remains remarkably open to the earth and sky. "From the outset," as Ken Taylor observes, "Canberra was envisaged as a city in the landscape and of the landscape."[4] The importance attributed to the natural environment of the planned city, an importance grounded in a new sense of Australian national identity, is evident in the competition announced in December 1912 for paintings depicting the federal capital site. The prize-winning entry was painted by William Lister Lister, but the runner-up, by Theodore Penleigh Boyd, is more frequently reproduced. It shows the Limestone Plains as an open expanse of grassland with three beautiful pale-barked gums in the foreground, intersected by two waterways, and ringed by forested hills, with the picturesque vista of a grander mountain range against the horizon. The lone church of St John the Baptist, shadowed by conifers, together with the suggestion of willows along the river bank, signals that this is a place already blessed with the presence of a Christian civilisation, but as yet innocent of the ills of urban life. The apparent vacancy of the plain offers itself as an open space, in which the urban planner and landscape artist might combine to create, quasi *ex nihilo*, a new kind of city, at once grand and green, for the newly constituted settler nation.

It is that vacancy, though, that worries me, for it was in fact illusory. The Aboriginal people who had lovingly shaped and maintained a "nourishing terrain" for themselves here over the millennia, together with many of the plants and animals that sustained them, had been decimated by white settlement in the course of the previous century.[5] In the meantime, though, the Limestone Plains had become a relatively nourishing terrain of a new sort for the recent arrivals themselves. The absence of stock and dwellings in this painting is suggestive of the ease with which the creators of the federal capital would suppress any thought of the suffering that its construction might cause the inhabitants of this pastoral country as a consequence of their loss of place and livelihood: a suffering that continues to this day, as the growing suburbs of Canberra continue to consume ever more remnants of this rural world.[6] Moreover, it would appear that the impulse to create a city that was genuinely attuned to its natural environment, a true dwelling place, in Heideggerian terms, that artistically mediated Earth and World, seems to have always been in tension with a contrary impulse to take the given as a blank slate on which to create something entirely other, within which natural phenomena are reduced to the status of mere stage setting and decoration.[7] This modernist impulse to make it new is abundantly clear in a comment made by Senator Stanford Smith in a parliamentary debate prior to the selection of the Canberra site. In his view,

> If any town is selected as the federal capital site, it may be necessary to absolutely destroy it before we can lay out the federal capital on the beautiful lines on which I believe it is the intention of the people of Australia that the capital city should be established.[8]

As it turned out, no existing cities had to be razed to create the federal capital, but as already indicated, the productive pastoral landscape was, slowly at first, then with accelerating rapidity, progressively gobbled up by an ever-expanding suburbia.

Interestingly, this process is often construed in terms not only of aesthetic "improvement," but also of environmental restoration. John Edmund Gray, for example, credits T. C. G. Weston, the Officer-in-Charge of Afforestation and later City Planting in Canberra from 1913 to 1926, with "reversing, by afforestation planting and conservation measures, the existing degradation of the site's landscape."[9] By contrast with the experience of urbanisation in more leafy parts of the world, the construction of this city led to a dramatic increase in tree coverage, and possibly also to a net gain in biodiversity, at least vis-à-vis the "degraded" pastoral environment. Some might quibble, as indeed Griffin did, with the overwhelming preponderance of exotics over natives in Weston's plantings, but the range of native species that can thrive in Canberra's harsh environment is actually fairly restricted, as Weston discovered.[10] It seems likely that nostalgia played a role in the preference displayed by Canberra's avid tree planters for deciduous trees in particular. Yet there are also good practical grounds not to plant trees that are both highly flammable and inclined to drop large branches at the least notice in close proximity to dwellings. And there is also much to be said for the shade provided by deciduous trees in the summer, especially, perhaps, for pale-skinned types like myself. Besides, in the era of global warming, many trees are surely better than few, even if, like most Australians, they or their forbears came here from abroad.

Weston and his successor as Superindendant of Parks and Gardens, Lindsay Pryor (1944–1958), were well equipped to realise the vision of Canberra as a Garden City that John Sulman, Chairman of the Federal Capital Advisory Committee from 1921 to 1924, grafted on to Griffin's original design. Even after Canberra began to expand rapidly from the late 1950s, under the watchful gaze of the National Capital Development Corporation, the city's lush green suburbs continued to be interpenetrated with open parkland and forested mountains; even little hills, such as my modest Rocky Nob, were graciously let be. Yet something was unquestionably lost in this process. As Bernadette Hince remarks, the social reform agenda of the Garden City movement, of which Sulman was a key proponent in Australia, rapidly became eclipsed by the "theme of a middle class suburban nation on the rise."[11] Whereas Sulman remained true to the project of bridging the country-city divide in envisioning Canberra's public parks as a kind of commons, where "'one can roam at will, families can picnic, and cattle and sheep can graze,'"[12] in the end, they became places purely of recreation, and in some cases also conservation, but generally not a commons in the traditional sense. The vast majority of private gardens in Canberra are similarly recreational and ornamental: pleasing to the senses and refreshing to the spirit they may be, but, with the exception of the fruit trees and maybe the odd vegetable patch, these mini private parks are not particularly nourishing to the body.

By the 1960s, the strict separation between urban and productive land had become so entrenched in the mentality of most Canberrans that old Mr Russell's few cattle, which still shared the sparse grasses up on Red Hill with the kangaroos, were viewed as a passing anachronism; while our Italian neighbours' backyard farmlet was seen as altogether improper, if rather quaint, and quite probably illegal. Whereas Howard had envisaged a partially self-provisioning and community-oriented garden city, with people living close to their place of work, we have ended up with a highly individualised city, in which people take time out to tend their private parks, while commuting ever greater distances from the proliferating suburbs to earn their crust in urban offices. Moreover, whereas Weston's reafforestation efforts were primarily oriented towards conservation, the planting of fast-growing conifers in neat straight rows soon became a significant commercial venture on the margins of the city, providing nourishment only indirectly to those who made an income from these ecologically impoverished, and, as we have recently witnessed, disastrously flammable plantations.

To some extent, the tension between respectful attunement and aggressive transformation of the natural environment also marks the work of Walter Burley Griffin. It is often observed that Griffin's plans were intended to accommodate the city to its natural environment, especially with regard to its topography and to a considerable extent also its vegetation. However, the geometric layout of the formal heart of the city, which is characteristic of the neo-classical orientation of the City Beautiful movement, implicitly sets human rationality, and the power of the state, over against the irregularity of natural features of the landscape. Whatever else might have been at play in Griffin's design, including the possibility that it encrypts a sacred geometry based on crystalline forms, he appears to have shared the ocular-centrism of the discourse of the picturesque that underpinned the choice of the national capital site and shaped its development.[13] Within this discourse, the hills surrounding the city are construed as an "amphitheatre": that is, as a stage-setting for the main action of nation building, which was to be conducted by men of reason, going about their business in the artfully designed buildings below.

The extent to which Griffin's own judgments were swayed by such visual considerations is betrayed above all by his extraordinary "Coloured Hills" concept, whereby Mt Ainslie was to be planted out with yellow-flowering plants, such as broom and acacias, Red Hill with red-flowering plants, such as callistemon, Mugga Mugga with white-flowering plants, such as Eucalyptus cinerea, and Black Mountain, with pink and white-flowering plants, such as Japanese peaches, plums, cherries and almonds.[14] Weston was happy to begin putting this bizarre plan into action on Red Hill and Mugga Mugga, but sagely refrained from covering Black Mountain with blossoming fruit trees.

To me, this betrays an attitude that implicitly denies to nature its own autopoiesis by treating the land like a canvas upon which to achieve certain preconceived visual effects. This tendency is also implicit in the creation of an artificial lake to "unify" the city. Doubtless, the lake is very beautiful, and it has come to support a variety of wildlife, as well as providing further opportunities for human recreation, if, once again, not subsistence. Nor, apparently, was this the first time that the Molonglo had been blocked, as evidence of a prehistoric lakebed has been found on the flood plain. However, quite apart from the potential consequences downstream of reduced water flow, there were some who grieved for the disappearance of what had once been a lovely, if labile, river valley and the productive agricultural land that it supported.[15]

Although Canberra is indubitably a fine work of art, it seems that Earth and World have not quite come together here yet: not unlike the Camp Hill Sandstone that rests unconformably on the far more ancient State Circle Slate of Capital Hill, Canberra's middle-class suburbia sits rather incongruously side by side with the bits of bushland that have been allowed to persist within and around it.[16] Canberra is therefore a place of edges and abysses, where you can unexpectedly fall into a seeming wilderness of Earth, while being otherwise enclosed in an extremely tame World, which seems designed precisely to keep nature at bay. So that when the Earth erupts into this World, as erupt it will, it can be quite a rude shock.

Consider, for example, last year's bogong moth scandal at the new Parliament House: a building that itself bears witness to the eco-cultural contradictions besetting the creation of the national capital. Being built into the hillside is evidently meant to convey an intention not to lord it over the land, but to become assimilated to it. In the process, however, the hillside has been ravaged, and the straggly native vegetation on its surface replaced with a sward of neatly trimmed lawn: the ground under the feet of the good citizens who were until recently invited to walk democratically over the heads of the assembled parliamentarians beneath, is a false floor, which effectively distances them from the earth of this place. Rather than letting the hill be a hill by accommodating the building to its contours, the hill has been forced to accommodate the building: to me, this looks more like appropriation than attunement.

Last spring, this profoundly ambiguous building became the site of a double visitation. How proud our Prime Minister was to be able to play host to two such crucial power-holders on the world stage as Chinese Premier Hu and President George Bush, Jnr. Our security was watertight, and all would have been well, but, horror of horrors, just at that moment, Parliament was beset by a hoard of uninvited guests, fluttering in and around every damn window and door. Those mountains are all very well from a distance, resting attractively along the horizon, but all Canberra seeks to shut out their dark denizens when they flock to our city lights en route to their annual aestivation in alpine crevices and caves. And the 40,000 lights of Parliament House burn long and strong. Well, we couldn't have the delicate sensibilities of the foreign dignitaries offended by the sight of this foul pest, could we? Naturally, the window ledges were liberally sprayed with insecticide. For several days, gardeners were to be seen depositing the thousands of dead moths that littered the parliamentary grounds into large garbage bags. But then, it seems, they started finding dead birds as well, at least a dozen currawongs according to newspaper reports, and there was talk of a silent spring.

As far as I have been able to ascertain, it is still unclear why these birds died; but what troubles me more, is that we probably would not have heard of the poisoning of the moths, which turns out to be an annual event, if these more charismatic creatures had not been affected too. That this annual slaughter has not seemed newsworthy is suggestive of our continuing refusal to accept this country as a goodly place in which, truly, to dwell. Moreover, this refusal cannot be disconnected from the injustices perpetrated against Aboriginal Australians here, and elsewhere, since British settlement, and from our continuing failure to achieve reconciliation. For those injustices were in large part grounded in a prior failure to respect Aboriginal ways of knowing and practices of place-making: a failure that is enshrined in the concept of *terra nullius*. One of the ways that Canberrans are learning to free themselves from that false notion is by recalling that the moths that now descend upon Canberra as an undesired eruption of abject Earth hold a place of honour in the World of the Kamberri people. Today we are reminded of that World by the bogong totem poles on Acton peninsula; and, when the season is right, children on excursion to Namadgi National Park are encouraged to taste the moths themselves. Yet, evidently, we still cannot tolerate their invasion of our neat clean city streets. For my own part, I look forward to the day when the lights of Canberra are dimmed out of regard for these passing visitants, and dignitaries from abroad are invited, not to gaze upon the beauty of the Brindabellas from afar, but to taste of their bounty: then, perhaps, we might have made further steps towards reconciliation, both between indigenous and non-indigenous Australians, and between the latter and the land

Notes

1   I am grateful to the Humanities Research School at the ANU for providing me with the opportunity to initiate my research on the eco-cultural history of the Canberra region as a Visiting Research Fellow there last year.

2   Thanks to Angela Hume for an introductory lesson in geology.

3   Ann Jackson-Nakano, *The Kamberri. A History of Aboriginal Families in the ACT and Surrounds,* Aboriginal History Monograph 8 (Canberra, 2001) 166.

4   Ken Taylor, "Picturesque Visions of a Nation: Capital City in the Garden", *The New Federalist*, 3 (June 1999) 74–80; here, 79.

5   On Aboriginal land management in the Canberra area see: Bill Gammage, *Australia under Aboriginal Land Management. 15th Barry Andrews Memorial Lecture* (Canberra: Canberra University College, ADFA, 2002) 17–23. On Aboriginal views of land, see also Deborah Bird Rose, *Nourishing Terrains. Australian Aboriginal Views of Landscape and Wilderness* (Canberra: Australian Heritage Commission, 1996); with Sharon D'Amico, Nancy Daiyi, Kathy Deveraux, Margy Daiyi, Linda Ford and April Bright, *Country of the Heart: An Indigenous Australian Homeland* (Canberra: Aboriginal Studies Press, 2002).

6   See eg Megan Doherty, "Last click of the shears for Gungahlin's pioneer farmers", *The Canberra Times*, Nov. 8, 2003: 1.

7   On Earth and World, as mediated by the work of art, see Heidegger, "The Origin of the Work of Art" in *Poetry, Language, Thought*, trans. and ed. Albert Hofstadter (New York: Harper and Row, 1971). Heidegger uses the term Earth here to refer to what the Greeks called *physis*, autopoietic, or primordial, nature, as distinct from World, as created by human language, culture and technology. In his later work, Heidegger writes of the dwelling place as an artful interweaving of the Fourfold of Earth, Sky, Gods and Mortals: an interweaving embodied in the way we think, speak and build. See "Building, Dwelling, Thinking", in *Poetry, Language, Thought*.

8   Cit. Taylor, "Picturesque Visions", 77.

9   J. E. Gray, *T. C. G. Weston (1866–1935), Horticulturalist and Arboriculturalist. A critical review of his contribution to the establishment of the landscape foundations of Australia's*. PhD thesis (Canberra: University of Canberra, July 1999).

10 Gray cites a comment of Griffin's in a radio interview to the effect that the planting of exotics was 'a very great mistake. They are not so suitable, and they are not so beautiful. No tree equals the eucalypt for embellishing the landscape.' Cit, Gray, 121. However, that he himself was not well versed in what was botanically 'suitable' is indicated by his proposal to plant spotted gums, which, as Weston had to explain to

him, only grew in coastal regions. Gray, 137.

11 B. Hince, *A Pryor Commitment. Canberra's Public Landscape 1944–1958*. Master of Science thesis (Canberra: ANU, October 1993); "Consultant's Report to ACT Landscape Public Works and Services", p. 12.

12 Gray, 120.

13 The case for the Griffin's having encoded mystical designs into the layout of Canberra is made by Peter Proudfoot in *The Secret Plan of Canberra* (Sydney: UNSW Press, 1994).

14 Gray, 100.

15 Hince, 185–86.

16 Jon Cameron, "Beneath Capital Hill: The Unconformities of Place and Self", in Mark Tredinnick, ed., *A Place on Earth. An Anthology of Nature Writing from Australia and New Zealand* (Sydney: UNSW Press, 2003) 55–56.

ILINDA MARKOVA

A DOOR TO NOWHERE

unnamed ringbarked eroded by salinity hollow
an orphanage for birds and snakes discoloured and disfigured
    dry
black branches like claws or talons preying on the passing
    Time
        the tree is still there
breakable fragile its stump mutilated by the winds the droughts
and the sun a sad sculpture of dust and ashes
a ruin of a by-gone civilisation   a ruin as important in the
context of nature as the Coliseum in Rome or the Parthenon in
Ancient Greece

        the tree is still there

like a hieroglyph for eternity written in Indian ink against the
red soil of a harsh landscape full of danger graphically
    beautiful
and ugly with history like this one:
It was in this tree that J. Wells was found after robbing
the Cunnamulla branch of the Queensland National Bank in
    1882

        the tree is still there

never to be used for paper or to heat a homestead it will
    remain
a humble friend of skinks and spiders that climb it as a ladder
    to
get nearer the sun where eagles are the soaring guards of a
    barren
sky   there was no rain for months sometimes for years
    dingoes
came and licked it in search of sap and moisture Its roots were
still alive and digging deep down desperate for water doomed
    It
was once a Christmas tree for a farmer and his wife but they
    are
no more around the drought chased them away long ago

the tree is still there

like a decaying tooth in the mouth of the horizon   a spirit of a
tree without constitution chopped down hurt by men
       immune to age
and pain it's still there like a sphinx among spinifex   it
remembers: when it was young and innocent a boy came and
       cut two
letters in its trunk encircled by a heart as big as a bull's an
arrow sharper than the knife piercing the heart   A small creek
 at its foot then was a waterhole for wild animals and cattle
A medicine man would occasionally come and take a piece of
       its
bark for a healing purpose chanting sacred words calling the
spirit of Mother Earth for help

the tree is still there

and has its conversations with the stars that love it the way
it is grotesque burned by bush fires salinity and the sun
The stars love the way it dances like a crane   its joints
squeaking in the wind like hinges of a door to nowhere

the tree is still there

standing like an urn   an unanimated structure   but for a tiny
sprout like a baby in a pouch—a green twig with
       a small green leaf is showing out

A BROLGA SONG

When it's raining I can hear my own people crying
crying far North
I can't wait to go home, take my shoes off and touch
the Earth which is my mum
my old mum
who taught me the didgeridoo

The man wiped his mouth
with the back of his hand and started playing
The phallic instrument sucked in his voice
whirled it around pushing it down down to deep and rich
bass sounds like thunder rattling away
(or was it a mob of kangaroos galloping?)
building up
building up
tension and suspense anticipation of danger lurking in the
shadows, in the haze, in the sand
under the rocks, under the sun ready to brand
your white out-of-place skin

Suddenly a syncope
the howl of wounded dingoes
bulls roaring stomping in fright or in a fight
Suddenly a dry hollow sound
drown by playful waterfalls in a
rainforest winds blowing across the canopy
magnified sounds of insects making love
sand grains running through the fingers of a child
whispering twenty words for sand suggesting colour
consistency pelt
transposed in music

dark mythical reverberating piercing lunatic
dancing on a razor blade innocent naive native
Suddenly a brolga song
                a sad brolga song saying
Nature's a song   man's a song
     woman is a walking bleeding song

CHAIN REACTION

what Galapagos and the tortoise Harriet were for young
Darwin what the hanging gardens of Semiramidis and the
tower were for Babylon what the spear was for the Zulu
warrior what the clay tablets of cuneiform writing
were for the book lover what Orpheus and his lyre were
for the beasts what the beauty of the vibrant coloured
plumage and the luring songs were for the mating birds
what Ned Kelly and his gang were for legend tellers what
the spill of blood of a sacrificed animal or child was
for the Egyptian priest what the feng shui compass and
the dragon's breath were for the Chinese geomant what
the trained blindfolded brown falcon was for the Uzbek
hunter what the medicine bag with feathers bones and
pebbles was for the shaman what snow was for the huskies
towing a sledge in pairs along the Pole Cap what
Columbus and the Grand Armada were for Spain what a royal
flush was for the poker gambler what the leather whip was
for Marquise de Sade or the "cat-o'-nine-tails" for the
order on a sailing ship what the ceremonial penis gourds
were for the Dani men what the camel train and the Silk
Road were for Marco Polo what the male praying-mantis was
for his female what life was to death   what

WALTZING MATILDA

We stand in a semicircle
a bunch of hermit-crabs after a new cone-shell
for families and friends we are house hunting
A flabby man in a black suit holding a wooden
hammer is tongue-twisting   *three bedrooms*
two bathrooms timber kitchen shed granny flat
his voice trained for a hiccup opening
accentuation
Hup two hundred eighteen thousand what'd you say
Hup two hundred twenty thousand in the back
Hup two hundred twenty one
While the auction goes we feel exposed in the open
as we all are crustaceans crawled out of our shells

houses cars caravans and office rooms
trying to find a new cone-shell to move in for
the next
Hup two hundred twenty eight thousands
years
is now the price give me yours
fake crustaceans   we want
something special perhaps a nice shell   named
Mathilda ... elegans or *Pyramidella ... pharaonius*
The hammer hiccups against the anvil of the sun
First time   Second time   Done

EINSTEIN & THE SWAGMAN

the pelican
the swagman of the lake is grooming feathers

it's one of those days that gives you a hug like
a classmate you haven't poked in the ribs for years
ripples on the surface
a mild breeze
a current
cormorants
flying under water to catch a meal
quietness
the trees stand solemn
the trees stand still
looking down at the mirror image of
clouds passing by
hand in hand with time
the trees   a bunch of Narcissuses
contemplate reflections of their
leaves and branches
intertwine with the canopy of water
plants and lilies to create
a feeling
where real and unreal blend

WORD EXERCISE NO 1

        the forbidden fruit
           the other name of sin
the apple Eve offered to her rib share-holder Adam
the poisoned apple the step-mother gave to Snow White
the apple Newton saw falling on the ground in his orchard
(year 1665, month of August: "there must be a force
that acts on the apple to cause its acceleration
 this force
     is
         gravity")
they forced William Tell to shoot an apple
  off his son's head with a crossbow
witches say apple has magic powers to bring love
procure healing   immortality
two apples the inevitable desert of the one-dollar dinner
at the men's hostel where they fight over fags and sickly
         whores
don't upset Bernard Shaw's *Apple Cart*
apple the symbol of New York
the Apple Market of Amsterdam where Rembrandt
loved to linger
         Apple Computer system
Apfel Strudel   apple pie
cider applejack calvados the favourite disinfectant of
        Dr Ravick
and the lost generation of perpetual emigrants
    pommes de terre   love apples
Cezanne painted green apples, Henri Matisse painted
Still Life With Apples leaving a discordant feeling
   of im b ala n ce
dishes full of apples offerings to the Gods in Egypt
you're the apple of my eye
        it's a pity I don't know you

MICAELA SAHHAR

WILLIAMSTOWN

An ancient Viking re-creation is locked up on the waterfront. Glammed up for the tourists. With a mythical dragon-bird head, this warship is artificial migration. In the 50s, when small town white picket fencers starting crowing about reffos sticking the country till it rolled belly-up, the image wasn't so sharp. They weren't the only ones coming out this way though. Williamstown was a siren—spreadeagled around the bay. It's still in the chasm between housing estate and slick restaurants—both mushrooms in their way—on Nelson Place, or the ornamental Tudor House garden on Electra next to a hive of vegetable industry.

Approaching Willy on a train that yawns into stations because everything's looser this way—its panorama begins in the scrawl of industrial ribbed buildings and cargo-crate stacks. But I reckon over the next decade or so even the not-Willy parts will be prime and "it's a bit Western Suburbs" won't insult the cut of your low slung tops.

Seagull: this is a bastardised name. It is harsh. Not a shred of their slivery silver gull origins.

Kee-ar—Kee-ar—Ka-aaar!

It is harsh. Out here in the Westgate's shadow their mouths are filled with tit-bits the tide turns up: dead or alive. Some say their time is wasted in snatching and squalling among themselves. This is an urban myth—they keep close counsel. Heads turned into their chests. Backs up with the cold, gran used to say, but birds can be greedy things. And they sulk by the military canons when the scrum hasn't gone their way. Elsewhere they're just pariahs taking pot-shots at market produce, but on the western side of the Bridge the gull is a cult. The fish and chippery at the corner of Ferguson Street has a proud slanty-eyed seagull with a peaky beak and stretched wings. It's at least three times bigger than the real ones who snakily flock across the road. Those canny things know sea air makes us order newspaper knots leaking chips, and they do a fair trade by the picnic benches any day of the week.

From the corner where Electra runs into Ferguson down to Nelson Place council diggers have stripped back the streets to a grid of pipes. A warning to pedestrians: look right. Down that way there's an information booth and flash new toilets if you're game to walk past a block of housing commission. The striped tape and orange netting are at half-mast after days of fierce wind. More tubing lolls next to witches' hats—a changing of the guards.

At low tide you can see the remains of Fort Gellibrand's famed seaward defence artillery. This is where barges off the penal hulks docked each morning to disembark their convict parties. State muscle had to be quick back then with their wily wards. Always looking to pull a crafty one in the slack of a moment. In 1855 it was the central battery of a system of fortification that stretched from the convict mustering yard between Gellibrand and Breakwater piers to out past the cricket ground. The military road to that outpost traces the rout of a wooden railway built by gangs along an embankment. Things took a turn when the Inspector-General of Penal Establishments was fatally assaulted by a candid party of convicts, revolting over watery prisons and relentless grind.

Swan: a chameleon thing. Head rigged up like a snake. Arced neck it looms with a hiss from a shallow drain. Back on the waves she puckers her bill.

They say a white-whiskered gentleman appeared in the final throws of the penal regime on a ferry from across the bay. He came every day for two years to watch the gangs at work before fading from documented view. His ferryman, a blade of few wits, gleaned nothing but his fair and the slip of a tenner on their last trip. By that time the Hulks housed ladies mostly, so make what you will of it.

Comings and goings are quick. They built that Viking prow lickety-split before a story was confirmed. When local memory, a disorderly beast, failed to cook up a headliner, some journo got wind of the ruck and advanced his sensational theory: Ancient Wreckage Unearthed at Newport. No question the find was a Viking long ship. But strenuous testing revealed they were just charred hulks, forgotten under the silt.

Now C. Blunt Boat Builder has berthed it at the back of the workshop behind a stuffed dumpster and snaggly trench-grade barbed wire.

The mechanics of Gellibrand's Hulks were dismantled in fits and starts. The Fort became a ghostland, overshadowed by its disreputable past. The President, a kangaroo palace for gents was gutted by 1860. The last, *Sacramento,* for visceral senoritas ditched 1878. They were let lie for years until someone finally insisted the old things were busted up for burning and towed to Newport's Greenwich Bay.

Mynah: buffoon with spread feet on corrugate iron—tipping his bigtop body about. An idler with time for gusty debate, throwing hectoring gurgles to his mate.

The United Friendly Society Dispensary, established 1876, gave a community feel to the place. Maybe this is what it lacked back then with an expectant air in the over-wide streets and magisterial shop fronts. When the area was first settled the planners envisaged Willy as the city's hub. But swampland and bad drainage made it all too hard, and for years it was just an overdressed suburban tendril on the skirts of Melbourne. Pharmacists are touchstones—no other profession doles out over-the-counter advice for free. The tone was set by the UFS's founder who dispensed there, uninterrupted, for forty years. It is no mean thing to roll your sleeves up into the same repetitive tasks. The work is not cumulative, although the reputation is, and not many people are cut out for it.

When picnics next to swings that levered over the sea became ritual, my grandmother insisted on putting up a fine spread packed from her kitchen. Dad stopped buying us fish-bits hotly bursting out of their batter in grease-speckled paper. The gulls weren't much into the hard little felafels ground from chickpeas or the crumbly tabouleh that wouldn't hold together in too thin bread and slopped into paper plates then swilled into my lap but not out again. Gran ended the meal flicking crumbs off our rug. The gulls would dash helter-skelter in every other direction: full up! she'd cry—satisfied that someone was and knew it.

Even at nine, when the sea seemed to mirror the sky, grim things could lurk on the undulating inverse horizon line. I never found starfish—hadn't the patience—but I had a knack with rubbish. The soft heap of a gull—slack necked and wound up in six-pack-plastic—was my crowning find. Wet and glassy and stiff, it was the only time I ever caught one. They can be hard little buggers to pin down.

Chook: shuffle kick. Shuffle peck. It wasn't so long ago the wreckers removed gran's coop, painted green to cheer it up. Although the wire was shot and the lower slats had fallen in.

Compound mixtures and creams were still staples of the 1960s script pad. Swabbed, folded and stirred on glass sheets with spatulas, or ground with the pounding twist of pestle on mortar. Chemists would knock anything up in under fifteen minutes. Grandma says dad wanted to do this always—an ambition that stretched back further than he remembers. But the youngest son in a house of seventeen, at cheek-by-jowl quarters, was easily womanised: chopping herbs, crushing grains into paste. Chores for a boy whose backbone hadn't hardened yet.

What sticks with Gran are domestic arrangements. She can't describe a streetscape of the 1950s, but she's lucid about the Holy Land (childhood in Bethlehem). She's lucid about stuffing eggplant with walnuts (on a three-legged stool) for pickling. In the original kitchen where the floor was black and my grandma trod the old boards until they broke, Pa would often exclaim "take it easy Ellen!" as her methodical feet took out the flaking wood structure in pieces. Lucky they were silly young things back then or they'd never have coped. Before street maps were cheap she remembers only that Pa would drive across the city to visit their married daughter: jogging his car in a side street until the number 5 tram lurched past. It's spindly mechanical arm as unreliable as the split record needle grandma wouldn't replace back in their Newport living room. Pa would never venture off his home patch without the lugubrious tilt of the tram. Like driving music in the days before car radios were installed. The noises he knew were factory ones. Chooks in the backyard. The scrabble of business between Spotswood, Newport and the Williamstown docks.

The Time Ball Tower set the tone for sonorous Williamstown. A light for shippers began as flame in a barrel held aloft on a staff. Later they built a wooden tower and hitched up an oil lamp. But the bluster of port weather and boom of the trade were decisive in pitching a bluestone tower in 1852. It takes its name from the impossible copper ball, hoisted by a system of pulleys day in and day out, lowered at 1pm for disorientated shipmasters. That lumbering time ball roared until the 20s when they farmed it out for newer methods.

There's a sense that people grow old in this place. Waiting it out on the sand. In recent years progressive pharmacies, trying to shark out the UFS, have organised systems for savvy pensioners. Dossett runs: the meals-on-wheels of medication. But the competition isn't really so fierce. My grandmother is not easily swayed by a smart buck—she's bound by the invisible tendon of old dealings.

Visiting grandma in her corner block at Merle Street, I was humiliated by the graffiti raw slats of her wood and tin fence backing onto an old VFL ground. Before the new Hobson Council pruned the fig to a hulk—transforming wild migrant orchards into sculpted prides of the bay—dad and his little sister would sit on that crooked fat thumb of a fig tree on Sunday mornings dodging the ground fee. On their laps, gran spread platefuls of misshapen chips: a matt-finished treat to save bad potatoes. My gaggle of migrants could save anything in those days if they turned their minds to it. The thriftiest boat-wives knew to send their children down to the butcher after hours. Sad, surly men sluicing blood off the tiles would bundle them up the spoiling trays. They knew what it was to clutch at straws. But forty years on those cuts come at a higher premium. Savvy Australia has learnt how to market the package: bill to claw.

Pelican: his bill's too full to speak. But that cad'll thrash at the sea-skin to roundup fish.

There's an older smell around these streets. Thrashed up in the road work on Ferguson. Like sniffing an old man's armpit or the Old Spice and cigarette that laces split wood in a doorjamb. Even the smart-as-paint boulevards are watched by factory smokestacks. A make-over won't shake those eyes of omnipotence. The one that sticks in my head has two red stripes and a white around the brim. You can see it from the Westgate also—a sentinel of the port that winks in the night to warn off low crafts. If you screw your eyes tight those lights are rough little jewels you could drag out of the dark. But only if you wind the car window back quick.

If you've been on a weekday in winter the new galleries are closed and the ice-creamery looks wistfully at the bleak industrial ships that swamp the port. There was a struggle along Nelson Place for years. At one time it seemed the ice-cream shop was there by happy coincidence—squatting inelegantly over half of an unfitted floor, with dubious opening hours and here today gone tomorrow fridges. Now, the lurid front has lost its surprise for a chalked up board of codified flavours. But if you'd seen it then, you'd know the good-bad-girls who used to live out this way were real women—none of your eastern skirt whose milky lives made medicine droppers and dummy clips of their tits. Game things who knew how to pulse, my aunts, since they played second fiddle to boys who would get degrees. They got the boys instead, dressed to kill in their sharp threads.

Pigeon: all kinds in the old roof. You could make a killing with a pretty pair of those in the Williamstown fifties.

Bad times and hard luck. These make for desperate people. Hotels mushroomed while thousands of migrants searched for a cheap roof until they were sorted. The quarters weren't flash—a hogshead of water never got anyone squeaky. Other things grew in the damp. Unlicensed drinking was quite a taboo: "The Bucket of Blood" was the first shanty recorded dispensing rum. Sly-grogging was rife. The authorities were keen to chalk up convictions and one was enough to black-ball a publican for life. But there were ways to make a quick bob that weren't an offence.

A hundred years later in the racket of Palestine's 1948 my grandparents scrimped from ground up. A bit of land and education were the stuff of their clipped dreams. Dipping into a textbook history of Willy, I read "in [the] early years [e]ducational requirements of Williamstown [w]ere served by private schools." But it was the public school system that advanced the refugee fable of the 1950s before state government vanquished this puncture in resources. Well, that's the story. For dad, the New World seal of graduation didn't swoop down from the sky like an answer. A boy for the birds, he remembers the gabling of a deserted house festooned with wild pigeons. Climbing up to their nests was always a thought, although he was mostly content with holding the heads of sick or abandoned ones until squeezing open their mouths they were fed with a dropper. He was sad to discover the Russian bloke on the corner was eating his hand-reared treasures, caged and sent by gran for a bob to make ends meet.

We recognise the end in retrospect. Those pigeons slowly leaked from the kitchen: detached from the house. Maybe when dad and his younger sister grew up and the others moved away so that slowly the gap between the tin roof and the wood of the walls hollowed out. When the external kitchen was demolished, grown weak from nesting and bird feet dad remarked how his pigeons had all disappeared. But migrants are tough chameleon things. Even in boats where the lower slats let water seep through they still caper a buffoon or two. They can nose out a racket before it breaks, rounding up kids in a masterful vanishing trick. My heirloom is an ephemeral thing that cannot describe the places where they have been. Touching them here the place unravels like a skein.

TOM GRIFFITHS

LEGEND AND LAMENT

In June 1863, Patsy Durack and John Costello, together with several men, a hundred horses and four hundred cattle, set off on a trek from Goulburn in New South Wales in search of an area of pastoral opportunity in south-western Queensland. About three months later they established a depot on the Paroo, back o' Bourke, and four of them pushed on with the cattle. The country was in the grip of drought. Dust-storms engulfed them, their horses fell in their tracks, and their cattle stampeded to drown in the last bog that smelt of water.

Facing death themselves, the pastoralists encountered a party of Aborigines "striding like lean giants through the waters of mirage". The blacks laid down their weapons and led the white men to a low, rocky outcrop and uncovered a well. They brought them grubs, goannas for roasting and little cakes of nardoo. Astonishingly, one of them spoke some English for he had helped John King, the only survivor of the exploring party of Burke and Wills of two years earlier. This Aboriginal man discouraged questioning about the land ahead, scowled and, pointing to the south, said 'Go! Go!'

But the pastoralists, encouraged by a flight of parrots to the north-west, which they hoped was an omen of water, decided to push on. They scavenged crows and kangaroo rats for food, but found no water. They did find, however, a half-buried packsaddle which they decided had been abandoned by Burke in his race for survival over the same plains. They called for help from the blacks whose fires they had seen, but none came. They shot their last horse and drank its blood.

Only then, desperate, did they turn back. At once the blacks reappeared. 'Go?' they confirmed. The Aboriginal men took them to another well in a limestone outcrop nearby, brought them more food, and over many days guided them back, via the hidden waters, to their depot and their white companions.

This is a distillation of Mary Durack's tale of her grandfather's first expedition into the outback in her classic family saga, *Kings in Grass Castles* (1959).[1] It is an astonishing story, on many levels. There is the compassionate but firm tutelage of the Aborigines. There is the bloody-minded (and dieted) determination of the pastoralists, their optimism proven by the fact that they soon returned, with wives and children, and established stations on the Cooper. There is the landscape of secrets and desire, of mirages and hidden waters, of omens both wishful and forbidding. There is the unambiguous assertion of ownership by the Aboriginal men. And there is the fact that Mary Durack tells the story at all, and does so with these cross-cultural nuances. For, as Pamela Lukin Watson describes in her book *Frontier Lands and Pioneer Legends* (1998), the story told by the son of the other expedition leader, John Costello, is quite different. It does record the disaster, but compares it to Napoleon's retreat from Moscow, omits any mention of Aborigines or even of other whites, and puts the survival down to John Costello's indomitable courage and resolve.[2]

This is the simplifying and corrupting power of legend, and "pioneer legends" are the subject of Watson's book. She analyses five pioneer accounts, all describing pastoral endeavours in the Channel Country near where the borders of Queensland, South Australia, New South Wales and the Northern Territory meet and where rain falling hundreds of kilometres away to the north east periodically floods down and over dry channels, bringing a spectacular pulse of life to the plains. This is also the land of the Karuwali, as well as of other Aboriginal peoples. The original currency of the country was pituri, a psychoactive drug made from the *Duboisia hopwoodii* bush which Aboriginal people traded up and down the rivers.

Three of the accounts studied by Watson in her book—those about John Costello, Robert Collins and Oscar de Satgé, all born a few years either side of 1840—conform to the pioneer legend as described by historian John Hirst in a famous essay published in 1978.[3] They are nationalist, conservative and nostalgic accounts of Australian settlement, which depict the pastoral pioneer as the hero in a battle with a hostile environment. Aborigines, if they figure in the legend at all, appear as one of the natural hazards with which the pioneer must contend. The power of this legend and the influence it has had on our history-making is now widely acknowledged, and so Watson directs our attention to two other accounts of the conquest of Karuwali land which break out of that mould in intriguing and challenging ways, and which now speak to our own times and sensibilities more directly. It is no coincidence that both the maverick accounts are by women: one is the source of the story above—Mary Durack's famous book about her grandfather—and the other is a far less well known series of memoirs by Alice Duncan-Kemp, who grew up in Karuwali country in the early twentieth century.

Both Durack and Duncan-Kemp provide more complex, satisfying and challenging frontier stories. The male pioneer pastoralists are revealed to be not alone but embedded in a network of immediate and extended family, and the land they seek to occupy is already owned and defended. The frontier is not merely elemental but cross-cultural; the pastoralists become economically dependent on the Aboriginal societies they encounter; their moral tenure is vulnerable, their environmental predicament fragile. "'Cattle Kings' ye call us," replied Patsy Durack in 1878, "then we are Kings in grass castles that may be blown away upon a puff of wind..."

Alice Duncan-Kemp's stories are the most intriguing.[4] In her books, *Our Sandhill Country* (1933), *Our Channel Country* (1962), *Where Strange Paths Go Down* (1964), and *Where Strange Gods Call* (1968), she describes life on the cattle station, Mooraberrie, managed by her father from 1894, and after his early death by her mother for another forty years. Alice was considered "fairly 'cracked' on the blacks" for she was immersed in their life from the time of her birth in about 1901, and she liked and admired them, taking special, empathetic interest in their spiritual beliefs. Even her style of storytelling is Aboriginal, for her narratives are woven around journeys in the landscape. When I visited the Channel Country in 2000, local pastoralists were still telling stories about Alice that emphasised her eccentricities and implicitly marginalised her testimony.

"Father believes that it is an uncontestable fact that Aborigines are the rightful owners", Alice Duncan-Kemp wrote, and it was William Duncan's habit to refer to two local elders as "the landlords". Mooraberrie was managed under the guidance, and with the grace, of the blacks; and it was a financial success at a time when many other properties failed. Aborigines determined where the homestead should be built, which sections of the property were accessible at particular seasons, and when cultural considerations should prevail over pastoral routines. They advised on weather forecasting, the likely extent of floods, natural signs of coming drought, where to find water, and the life cycle of grasses. Duncan-Kemp's memoirs are unusual indeed—they constitute one of the few documented instances of environmental lore crossing cultures, and being applied with cooperative respect, on an Australian pastoral station.

Work on the property, both pastoral and domestic, relied fully on the Aborigines. They were the best riders and horse-breakers, and knew where the cattle might be found and mustered in the vast territory. They built the homestead, established the gardens, and cleaned the house. They dug and cleaned wells; they fought bushfires; they branded cattle. Their pay was tea, tobacco, clothing and food: two bullocks were killed every month for the camp of 200 Aborigines. At grace before dinner the Duncan family recited their own kind of prayer, a daily, double acknowledgement: "White pioneers, black saviours".[5]

Here is a different version of the legend: the Aborigines and the pastoralists helped one another stay on "their" land. But Watson's book also tells, with regional variations, a now familiar but no less shocking national story of frontier wars, exploitation and disease. The Karuwali were shot, starved, raped, speared and kidnapped; sexual diseases were knowingly introduced by settlers and wrought havoc; massacres were planned and executed; Aboriginal people were removed from their land and families and put on reserves. We have hidden from ourselves the extent to which cattle stations were, from the beginning, to quote anthropologists Howard and Frances Morphy, "a mode of colonisation and expropriation, rather than viable business enterprises".[6] They were part of a speculative frontier of "map grazing", as it was called. Short-term environmental thinking was endemic. "Home", for the settler, was generally elsewhere. Sheep and cattle were "the shock troops of empire".[7] Journalist George Farwell recorded a settler near Cooper Creek claiming that he used to be able to stand on a hillock and see the flat beyond full of Aboriginal people with the women "as thick as sheep grazing" as they searched for seeds and roots. One nomadic, grazing animal had replaced another, seemed to be the settler's message. But the statement was also both testimony to the original density of Aboriginal occupation and a graphic symbol of dispossession by hoof.

"Black armband" histories are not modern-day rewrites; they were part of frontier talk, they were distilled in the records of the time, and they informed the thinking especially of educated people. Rather, it was the pioneer legend that was revisionist, argues Watson, obfuscating "the wealth of knowledge and controversy about pioneering which obviously existed in the nineteenth century". The story presented by Watson and embodied in Alice Duncan-Kemp's account portrays the pioneers as human but no less heroic: added to their elemental battles were those moral and emotional ones with "intelligent members of a culture that is both complex and alien", and on which their own success utterly depended.

Few squatters wrote about their relationships with Aboriginal employees, even though Mooraberrie was one of many stations in Queensland being worked almost entirely by Aborigines. And few whites publicly acknowledged the ways that Aborigines independently exploited the land for their own purposes. They had their reasons. The pioneer legend either totally denied the presence of blacks in a region or else depicted them as poor users of the land, thereby justifying white occupation by Aboriginal absence or default. "In contrast," writes Watson provocatively, "Duncan-Kemp's evidence indicates that if the degree of utilisation of land were to be taken as the sole criteria for awarding rights to possession, then there would have been better reasons for leaving it in black hands than granting it to squatters."

That insight still has the power to disturb us today. The winds of inland and northern Australia are blowing cold and hard for the kings in grass castles in the early twenty-first century. The cattle culture of the inland and north now survives, in many instances, on little more than hope and history. Legends both lured the distant investors and sustained the people on the ground; they still prop the industry up today, as the politics of Wik demonstrated in the late 1990s. Pastoralists developed a distinctive sub-culture, an heroic, conservative and defensive world-view. This was once a highly adaptive survival strategy, and one that helped settlers through times of environmental and economic stress. But it has become a handicap in an era of multiple uses of the rangelands, and of more complex politics of land.

The way in which we value the rangelands has been changing rapidly, away from commodity values and towards amenity values, away from pastoralism and towards tourism, recreation, biodiversity preservation and Aboriginal traditional and contemporary uses. This is a radical revaluation of resources, comparable perhaps with the way in which, in the 1970s, Australians began to reassess the economic, natural and recreational values of their forests.

Now it is the turn of the rangelands to move into the scientific and political limelight. Even the formal, scientific definition of "the rangelands" (originally an American term) has moved in the last ten years from being primarily about the stock they were expected to carry, to a purely ecological definition, invoking soils and climate. The settlers' certainty that these inland plains should be used by white pastoralists for grazing is crumbling in our own generation. It is not just that there is now greater recognition and accommodation of Aboriginal land rights; it is also that there is increasing visibility and valuation of conservation issues.

In fact the environmental issues are much more a cause of "uncertainty" in the pastoral industry than is native title. The real threats to pastoralists are "economic viability, land degradation, desertification, wildlife extinctions, threatened species, ecologically sustainable development and biodiversity", to quote CSIRO scientist, Steve Morton.[8] The rate of mammal extinctions in the Australian rangelands is already the highest in the world. And, as Morton points out, the plight of the native mammals is much more bound up with the declining fortunes of the graziers than is the rise of Aboriginal politics. But Aborigines have again become the scapegoat because they not only divert attention from the bitter economic and environmental realities of pastoralism in outback Australia, but also because evoking them as a threat revives the frontier mentality that has always underpinned the cattle culture. So, just as a museum such as the Stockman's Hall of Fame virtually ignores the environmental dimensions of the history of the rangelands, so did political debate about the Wik decision overlook its environmental background and implications.

In her book *Uncommon Ground: Cultural Landscapes and Environmental Values* (Oxford, 1997), British anthropologist Veronica Strang focused on two groups of people in the Mitchell river catchment area of Cape York Peninsula—white pastoralists and Aboriginal communities. One of the largest watersheds in Australia and just south of the country of the Wik people, the Mitchell River drains a fragile environment of easily eroded and infertile soils. The Aboriginal population is centred in the Gulf coastal community of Kowanyama, and the pastoralists are scattered through the catchment in small groups of three to twenty people on the cattle stations. The pattern of invasion is thus reversed, with the numerically dominant Aborigines mostly in the coastal settlement, and the graziers (only a few hundred of them) dispersed across territories or properties generally of more than one thousand square miles.

The distinction between "pastoralists" and "Aborigines" can, of course, be misleading. Not only have Aboriginal people been pastoral labourers, an increasing number of them are now owner-pastoralists themselves. In any case, European pastoralists were always more like the Aborigines than they themselves knew or could afford to recognise.

Livestock herding echoed aspects of kangaroo hunting, and both lacked the moral and social power of "agriculture". Pastoralism is, after all, a kind of domesticated hunting. It is systematic predation, it supports a low number of people relative to the space it requires, it is nomadic within bounded territories, it grapples with a fringe environment that threatens to become desert, and it employs fire as a farming tool. Cross-cultural parallels between the modes of production of pastoralists and Aborigines cause as much insecurity amongst settlers as do the differences. Unwanted similarity can itself prompt people to assert difference. Pastoralists sometimes worried about the Aboriginality of their economy.

Veronica Strang looks past these external, economic practices (which are "more form than substance") and analyses the underlying fundamentals, "the values and beliefs, the social and spiritual structures" of both Aborigines and pastoralists—and here she finds great contrasts. Strang begins her book with two accounts of the same place, Emu Lagoon, one through the perceptions, practices and stories of Aboriginal elders, and the other of the white owner-manager of a local pastoral station. "They can walk around the same water, scuff the same dust and sit under the same trees, but they are not in the same place", concludes the author.[9] She enables us to empathise with two completely different ways of being in the same land, and therefore to confront the emotional as well as the legal and practical challenges entailed in sharing the country.

In seeking to understand change in Aboriginal society, it is Strang's achievement to see beyond the Toyotas—so often a symbol of Aboriginal power, corruption and loss—and to divine the deep continuities that permeate Aboriginal stewardship of land in spite of recent social trauma and obvious economic and technological change. And pastoralists emerge, by contrast, as "somewhat more adrift". Even the period of colonial settlement, argues Strang, offered them more stability than is provided by the large-scale, urbanised and fast-changing society to which they are now tied. They "rode into the Gulf country on the momentum of modern Europe", and their culture's history of fragmentation, mobility and change—the tide that propelled them to this distant frontier—has now left them stranded, economically as well as emotionally. Even their society's reverence for lone, conquering heroes making their mark on the land, a legend that had once sustained them, is now under question. Their noble frontier is now regarded as a backwater (there are still no more people there than there ever was), they rarely have their own land for any length of time, and "their lives are full of strangers". Ironically, one of the "environmental values" that is beginning to be shared between Aboriginal people and some pastoralists on the Gulf is a strong sense of belonging to that land, and so there are graziers who want to stay, emotions overwhelming economics. But, as Deborah Rose has shown, it is the pastoralists' cultural burden to be harbingers of change, and therefore to be unable to imagine a future that is anything like their present.[10]

Veronica Strang finds a pastoral industry "in deep trouble", gripped by economic decline and self-doubt—and, by contrast, an Aboriginal culture that "is quietly re-establishing a solid and sustaining environmental relationship." She wryly reflects that, fifty years ago, the anthropologist Lauriston Sharp, after studying people in the same region, predicted the eventual demise of the Aboriginal people there. But by the end of the century, the tables had turned—and it is now the white pastoralists who are fighting extinction.

"We too have lost our dreaming" lamented Judith Wright when reflecting on her ancestors' eventual abandonment of pastoral lands in Queensland, a tale she told in two versions, first as *The Generations of Men* in 1959 and then as *The Cry for the Dead* in 1981. The second book expressed her discovery of the Aboriginal history of pastoralism, her own conscious reworking, as she put it, of the "Australian legend". Wright liked to think that the Duracks, on their great cattle trek, had passed near the land where, a few years later, her grandparents would establish their station, "Nulalbin", in the Dawson River valley, inland from Rockhampton.[11] Her ancestors shared Duncan-Kemp's sympathy with, and reliance on, Aboriginal people. *The Cry for the Dead* is a lament for those original people whose lands her forebears, however sympathetic, usurped. But the book is also a story of the swift dispossession of her own ancestors, the loss of Wright's stolen inheritance by "traders and stock-exchanges"—"what's stolen once is stolen again", she mused. In the debate on the Land Act of 1902, James Norton had asked "Where are the pioneers?", and he mourned that the country was fast passing into the hands of the mortgagees. In her poem "Two Dreamtimes" (1973), which was addressed to the Aboriginal poet Oodgeroo Noonuccal (Kath Walker), Judith Wright reflected that, although "a knife's between us", she and her black sister shared "grief for lost country... poisoned now and crumbling".

Aborigines have been forcibly removed from many pastoral

districts, and—for different reasons—so have some of the white settlers who remember that the blacks were actually once there with them, working the land. That double discontinuity, double dispossession, has allowed history to be rewritten and re-invented. "Modern pastoralists have a problem", writes Peter Read, "—a frightening ignorance of a history no older than their own grandparents."[12] Pamela Lukin Watson agrees: "Pastoralists themselves know less and less about the conditions under which the land they lease was seized from indigenous communities." Today's managers of "Mooraberrie", for example, have no awareness of the Karuwali, or of the fact that earlier lease-holders, William and Laura Duncan, regarded the blacks as their landlords, and depended financially and emotionally on their labour and environmental wisdom.

Sometimes as scholars and writers we mistakenly assume the power of literature and underestimate the gulf between popular and learned understandings of history. When Judith Wright was finishing *The Cry for the Dead* in the late 1970s, she and her daughter Meredith travelled to the Dawson River area to check final details. Wright did her best to present herself as "convincingly harmless" to locals because she was worried they would not speak to her, since her sympathies with Aboriginal people were well known. But the trip was a success and she "did [her] poodle-faking act very well", and Meredith "kept discreetly silent".[13] Last year I made a similar journey, travelling to the heart of Wadja country, and I took with me, as my gesture of acknowledgement to country, Wright's two books, *The Generations of Men* and *The Cry for the Dead*. They are still the only substantial published sources on the history of that particular land. I, too, was anxious about how to play the local politics, but keen to learn about the books' reception amongst their most important readers. I stayed a night on a farm on the very earth where Wright's forebears had paid their respects to the Aboriginal owners. I got these much-loved books out of my swag and passed them around amongst the contemporary residents of that country. No-one had ever heard of them.

Notes

1 Mary Durack, *Kings in Grass Castles* (1959, Sydney: Corgi Books, 1979) 87–91.

2 Pamela Lukin Watson, *Frontier Lands and Pioneer Legends: How pastoralists gained Karuwali land* (Sydney: Allen & Unwin, 1998).

3 J. B. Hirst, "The Pioneer Legend", *Historical Studies*, 18.71 (1978): 316–37.

4 For biographical background see Yvette Steinhauer, "A. M. Duncan-Kemp: Her Life and Work", *Journal of Australian Studies*, 67 (2001) 37–43.

5 Watson, 34; chap. 3.

6 Howard Morphy and Frances Morphy, "The spirit of the plains kangaroo", in Tim Bonyhady and Tom Griffiths, eds., *Words for Country: Landscape and Language in Australia* (Sydney: UNSW Press, 2002) 107.

7 Shaun Milton, "The Transvaal Beef Frontier: Environment, Markets and the Ideology of Development, 1902–1942", in Tom Griffiths and Libby Robin, eds., *Ecology and Empire: Environmental History of Settler Societies* (Edinburgh: Keele University Press, 1997) 199–212.

8 S. R. Morton, "Changing Conservation Perceptions in the Australian Rangelands", *Rangelands Journal*, 15.1 (1993) 145–53.

9 Veronica Strang, *Uncommon Ground: Cultural Landscapes and Environmental Values*, (Oxford: Berg, 1997) 4.

10 Deborah Rose, "The Year Zero and the North Australian Frontier", in D. B. Rose and A. Clarke, eds., *Tracking Knowledge in North Australian Landscapes: Studies in Indigenous and Settler Ecological Knowledge Systems* (Darwin: North Australia Research Unit, ANU, 1997) 19–36.

11 Veronica Brady, *South of My Days: A Biography of Judith Wright* (Sydney: HarperCollins) 179.

12 Peter Read, "Belonging, Sharing and the Wik Judgment", in *Australian Humanities Review* (1997).

13 Brady, 381–82.

JENNIFER HARRISON

THE SHARK

Shocked from your fishing perch,
surprised by the gulls' echoes of distress,
you retreat to the rock-wall.

Dawn slinks like a bright cat
along the sky's spine
and illuminates the quiet fin

arriving suddenly
to hunt for breame on the outgoing tide.
You retreat to watch from the rock-wall

glad that the shark is neither human
nor spawned by Azrael or Lilith;
glad that the melanous Maclean

weaves through corn and giant cane
and is loyal to its own—
ripple-waking the giant shadow

now visible
beneath the slicing silver fin.
Shocked from your fishing perch

you watch the pale limned cartilage
the triangle ruffling like ribbon—
softer, more casual

than you imagined it could be.
With intimate swish, it cruises
the deep eye of the river

turns slow-circle
and, now, as though surprised
by cormorants, black in massed flight,

slides silently away.
Dawn has slunk like a bright cat into the day.
Shocked from your fishing perch

you retreat to the bait-white wall.
Line-tangled, a plastic-green reel
within your reach, you think

of the children's game,
how two pictures seem the same
even though details make a difference:

(there are only two buttons
on the girl's windcheater
not three;

the boat returning from sea in the background
has disappeared)
the shark was never there.

New Road In
   —for Robyn

A road red as a flayed weal,
a clay scar pushing into the wilderness,
road I travelled once with you.

Road cut into the mountain's heart;
tunnel to the machines, their giant pistons
grinding ohms from tussock-bled water.

Gelignite has reminded ice
that ice is no longer the master of granite:
hydroelectric

trapped waterfall, the boiling power.
Sun falls softly on lakeside houses,
a tour guide's glacial bee droning towards infinity.

I imagine a waterfall turning back
towards sky, a discourse, rainbow-fractured—
a road unmaking itself

its scar backtracking to the pristine
to the piles of gouged earth
puzzled by tattoos of tractor tread

to healing—and a new road in,
an invisible one, archived by rain
lit by an explosion of borealis.

Come into this wilderness
as into a mirror or a film,
thicket green, ferns swaying

over brackens lisped by rain
mist rising from the Sound
where wild deer sip from streams

tasting of snow and lichen
where the Tasman licks
the stony tears of weathered precipices.

New road in, deeper now.
How will we know which way to go?
Who might guide us in such a place?

Was that echo true?
Months of wilderness—
road I travelled once with you.

LANDSCAPE

I
Offered as a souvenir
engraved with the name of an old harbour
I give you the red sky
that has bled so long though our words.

These are the doorways of home
one front one back
and the hall of anxiety between
roped as though we might fall.

We swing such heavy anchors
as we strain at the tide
each night drifting drifting
like a Papuan moon.

II
Unconscious these melodies.
Where do they come from
and why so diffuse? I am
lacking in substance

and must lacquer the news.
Dogs lounge and yawn
then stiffly move.
And so must I refuse
the half-improvised sketch

which would leave me more armour.
Magic's trick with words
is not the hushed or fabled crime
but what's confessed behind.

III
If we'd known how
to singe the shadow, the cliché, the dream
without burning, we would have driven
that flame to its ash.

These insights I style acrylic/ally
are cities though less than a match
broken before lit. They are Plath's
brass balls. The ones she juggled best

above water, above trains thundering
along rifle-slick steel, above the heart's
apartments that glow and pulse
escaping the wonder of their forms.

IV
One knee bent, the other extended.
Why should I curtsey?
We can't reclaim the ship, the wisp of hair
although we dredge the ruined bay for combs.

When the statue in the mall
hands me his frozen rose,
I think of slender colours, lunar rubble
and of Gozzi's *Turandot*.

But this is the port I return to,
capriciously, as though I must remain
forever bound to the taken breast, though
where it went I cannot know, or say.

LOUISE CRISP

DASYURUS MACULATUS

    in the midst of iron wood:
    the disjunct grove

    mottle shadows slide past
    into the sun on the rocks

    glossy leaves draw me down
    to the head of the dry creek

    I look for a trace of pelt—
    rubbing the small depressions

    of the trunk where claw marks
    climb to the highest branches

    there's a place to feast & dangle
    a spotted tail

    to look out over the hills
    for relatives extinct or across the water

Note

Dasyurus maculatus, Spot-tailed quoll or Tiger Quoll
Eucalyptus maculata, Spotted Gum or Spotted Iron Gum

JUDITH BEVERIDGE

McKINNON'S BAY

She had heard the cormorants' defensive cries, and through
her binoculars saw the jaegars circling the skies before they
swooped in for the chicks. The wind was shunting in a heavy
storm, so she searched for him along the cliffs. He was
    tucked
into a crevice of the storm-quarried rocks, still tracking petrels
and albatross, his red jacket inflated by wind like a
    frigatebird's
puffed-out throat; the lightning falling like wind-whipped
streamers moulted from a flock of tropic birds, the sky
    roiling,
the thunder as guttural as those cries from the breeding ledges
where cormorants were guarding their chicks.... She returns

each year to the site. Above the pier, hawks and gannets
still find amplitude on the air-currents; the yachts race as if
they were quills trying to ratify documents. Still, the water
washes his name into her ears, sets spray against her legs
like the windblown news.... Holding her binoculars to the
    rocks,
she sees the cormorants, hundreds of them, still pillorying
their wings to an invisible framework of wind, exposed like
offenders to the derision of the weather and the skuas who
still come in for the chicks.... Her binoculars feel as heavy
as the legs of oil-burdened birds seeking purchase on a place

that's nothing but wind, droppings, and slipping scree. Above
the crags albatross circle to a point of stall, glide to turn
    steeply
at right angles across the bay.... Always he'd be there on the
ledges watching, as they'd soar around the cliff, catching
    updrafts.
For so long she thought she still saw him along the skyline:
ghost-written by spray, holding a wounded bird, gently
    twisting
the pain from its legs, still searching the sky for its raucous
storyline.... They found his jacket floating like a marker buoy;
later, his body washed up: his eyes, fingers, and toes already
gone to the crabs. Still her binoculars hold those birds caught

like sand grains in the weary throat of time…. Still the circles
draw no closer in; his face always retreating in the folding
   light,
no matter how much she turns the focus wheel; everything
moving across that span of sky, a circle that never closes
but constantly sweeps away… "Albatross can ride the currents
for hours, rarely needing to flap their wings," he'd tell her.
"They can stabilise themselves with their webbed feet which
act as airbrakes if they come in to alight on the ledges."… She
thinks again of his red jacket ballooning out in the wind; a
mocking, deadly display—just as he slips from the rocks.

BARBARA HOLLOWAY

THE LOGIC OF BIRDS

Bee-eater
Blue wrens
Chough
Currawong
Diamond firetail
Dollar bird
Double-barred finch
Eastern Spinebill
Fairy martin
Firetails
Friar-bird
Grey fantail
Grey thrush
Honey eaters:
      Black-chinned
      White-cheeked
      White-faced
      Yellow cheeked
      White Plumed
Mistletoe bird
Parrot: rosella
Parrot: superb
Peaceful dove
Pied butcher bird
Quail—button?
Rufous fantail
Rufous whistler
Sacred Kingfisher
Southern whiteface

More than one in ten animals and plants are already doomed because it will take decades to undo the global warming gases already in the atmosphere. The first major assessment of the effect of climate change on six biologically rich regions of the world, including one in Australia, showed that species living in mountainous areas had a greater chance of survival because they could move uphill to get cooler. Birds, able to fly, had the greatest chance of escape uphill, but that doesn't take into account that trees and other habitat they need for species survival will not move or change rapidly, "and all would die". "What we found we wish we had not": it may be an underestimate. (*Nature*, 7–14 January, 2004).

From my stump in the early morning air, I watch them at the bird bath. Is it you or you or you? And you. Let the modelling be wrong.

> Speckled warbler
> Spotted pardalote
> Striated pardalote
> Tawny frogmouth
> Top-knot pigeon
> Wattlebird
> Welcome swallow
> White capped robin
> White-browed babblers
> White-throated tree creeper
> Willy wagtail
> Yellow robin
> Yellow thornbill

Most avian species cannot do more than bluff their way to safety.

The flock of greenleeks flew up between the hot headstones and landed again among the Protestants. They strutted into grass bleached by early summer, twittering to each other, seizing seedheads and turning up dust with their gnarled feet.

I was hunting for my great-uncle. I found his parents' tombstone, fallen over in the space of first burials, the Masons' symbol prominent, no cross. I stood under the blazing sun squinting at the dates and German names that give away their flight from Austro-Hungarian intolerances.

Their son, my uncle, went from farm to farm inspecting and buying wheat for his employer, Connolly's Flours. His old docket books itemise his expenses, the cost of a ticket to take his bicycle on the train each week as he moved between the centres. I see him getting his bike from the goods van and pedalling gravely along tracks and lanes between the farms, 10 km, 15 km, under pressure to get there before reps from other mills.

There was no sign of a headstone for this old bachelor I can hardly remember, and the greenleeks found the pickings slim among the long-dead. They took off for seedier unconsecrated ground beyond the fence. I went back to the house I was renting in a paddock in the flat wheat lands.

In dry wind unbroken by landform or vegetation for many kilometres, a young crow was trying to land on a solitary stringybark. Making a circuit to a branch, it misjudged the wind and missed entirely. Still airborne, it made a second run, turned to the tree, beating and clutching with its claws at the bark of the trunk, but, still flapping, it was torn away by the wind. It fell on the ground the other side of the fence, silent, feathers ruffed up by the hurtling air. The yellow round its beak, like a clown's mouth, showed that although it had full feathers, it had not long been responsible for itself. Flying, like walking and singing, is a learned art.

> Feathers of wing can withstand immense air pressure during flight without being torn apart. Each feather is a separate unit but gaps may also occur between strands of a single feather. Each strand has small barbs which intermesh with barbs and smaller branches of the next strand of the feather. While light in weight, these hooked cross-connections cling together so strongly that they prevent air from ripping them apart in flight.

Birds flew long before humans walked. Birds sang long before people talked. The oldest fossil of a songbird has been dated at 54 million years by geologists. These fossilised bones were found in south-eastern Queensland and in fact there is evidence suggesting that unlike humans and most animals, songbirds actually first evolved on the Australian area of Gwondanaland, and spread north from here. Corvidae (crows), too. Other birds, though, came south from the Northern Hemisphere over the millenia.

It is the bigger flock birds, the grain eaters, that flourish in graingrowing country now. When I first got there, it was a hard winter after an extra hot summer. Not yet the full drought, but no wild seed was left. Crowds of greenleeks and ring-necks and red-rumps flew up and down for the grain dribbled from the truck that crawled past to feed the sheep. Others balanced overhead in couples on the power lines. Blue-bonnets hung upsidedown by one foot from the ringlock fence round the house, reaching for thistle-heads they took with a psittecaceous snip and tore apart.

Galahs cruised the wintry sky in crowds, moving fragments of a smooth cloud that wheeled, flashing sunset or dawn as they turned up their rosy bellies.

> Therewith a wind, scarcely stirring,
> Made in the green leaves a noise soft
> According to the birds' aloft song.

It finally rained in the spring, and the parrots disappeared in pairs to nest round the lanes and paddock edges. At night during the cold months, a long and secretive cry haunted the dark, answered by another. It must be a bird, sometimes quite near, sometimes far off, but what bird could sound like this?

Walking through new grass one afternoon I glimpsed, I thought, a hare, which turned into a bird about that height, crouching head-forward, frozen for camouflage. I should walk away, I told myself, and not disturb it. But curiosity is very powerful. I walked towards it. When it judged I had come dangerously close, it opened large wings and flew awkwardly, just above the grass, landing a hundred metres away. Its patterned tawny wings were far longer than the body suggested. Its mate suddenly moved. It ran head forward, like someone fleeing the police, and jumped a fence. I stifled the urge to make them fly again.

Since there was no picture of outspread wings in the bird books, there wasn't much to go on, and all my iconic eye had on its screen was the head. The farm owner didn't know; he has few names for local things.

After weeks of hearing and asking after this strange voice, with occasional distant sightings, I worked out it was "the stone curlew, known as thick-knees". Its Wiradgeri name is *willaroo*. That name comes closest to its call and its beautiful wings. The bird is on the endangered species list because its grasslands get smaller and smaller and smaller, it lives and nests on the ground, and it's a poor flier. How can anyone call it thick-knees?

What you hope is for the bird to live a little bit in one end of its name, and that you enter the other end and experience something of the bird in the word it is called by.

Those wings. Whose cries, calls and twitters.

A small songbird may have 1000 feathers while a large bird, such as a swan, can have more than 25 000. (9)

It rained enough for a new season's grasses to seed. The sky pressed down harder each day, crops flourished, then dried to gold and bleached white. Snakes and goannas came out, and the ants, but few birds. There were never any small birds there, no wrens, finches, weebills and wagtails. There is no bush understorey left. Little company, except, yes, the Apostle Birds.

To a solitary human, the Apostle Birds seem very sociable. Smart dark grey with black and tan touches, Apostle Birds hang in groups. They move together and chat in low tones constantly. So when the last puddle dried up I put water out. The flock came round, looked, and passed on whistling and clicking to each other. A few hours later they came back. I laughed as they started to see what a good thing a water bowl was, standing on the edge, jumping in and fluffing madly, bouncing off and out and in again, whistling and chirruping. I wanted to understand their talk with each other. In one mad moment I thought I might be able to speak it too. They flew off when I went to the door, however smoothly I moved.

There were foxes, a feral cat, and new neighbours ploughing and spraying ever closer to the fence lines. Filling the water bowl one last time, I packed and left grainland, left my great-uncle's tracks and non-conforming great-grandparents under their fallen tombstone.

I needed somewhere with small birds, a place where it didn't feel like rural development was about to wipe out the poor remains.

Bird wings and song are a sign of the intangible spirit in many cultures and religions.

Two years later I found and bought a block of cheap, 'useless' slope of the Crowther Range, in Wiradgeri country. Human neighbours are invisible, but birds of every size and habit throng the air and the forest and the neighbourhood. It could be called Wing City.

The soil is loose, washed downhill or blown over rock and stones from the cultivated flat paddocks stretching as far as you can see west across an ancient swamp. Birds that tunnel and burrow into the ground for nesting favour the place: bee-eaters, dollar-birds and kingfishers. There is a small house. At night the sound of a wallaby steadily crunching pine needles drifts in the windows. Because there are wallabies, there is no garden. There have been huge trees here, their charred circles still in the ground, a wood so hard it hasn't rotted in a century nor been devoured by the rampant termites. There are echidnas, who push the rocks around in search for ants, then take turns to climb up and cool off in the bird bath. The lower slope is dense indigenous cypress pine—in weed quantities after all the ringbarking and burning and grazing—but there are still good numbers of ironbarks and blood-woods, stringybark, blakelyi, and a eucalypt I don't know scattered among the pine. The bigger trees have a skirt of rocks that the growing trunk has pushed up. Long walls of lichened stones have been heaped up by past owners.

In the morning, eastern greys and wallaroos come down between the trees to the grass-slopes where they feed and lie between the tussocks in the sun.

In this drought the permanent water is a creek a way off. I keep two water bowls full by the house and sit on a stump, filming small birds. They arrive each morning, every morning to party just as the sun reaches the tree over the water. All mixes of honeyeaters, wrens, robins, fantails, pardalotes and finches flip into the branches, flip down, pause, chase each other through the twigs, round the clearing, back to the water, jump in and splash wildly, jump out, repeat.

Nothing is more difficult to film and identify than a small bird fresh from the bath, ruffled, damp, and chirpy. Sip, look over right shoulder, left shoulder, sip, up onto branch, jump down, left and right shoulder, jump into water entirely, quick full-feather-fluff-flurry of a bath, out, up to tree top. Mate comes down, both drink again, both doing left-right shoulder routine. Into tree, one pulls a long casuarina-needle through her beak as if cleaning her teeth, the final touch. They take off together again performing complex figures together between branches, out-down either side of tree having one last sip and flying off for the day.

The raised wing of any bird, glimpsed from below is almost naked. The bones are outlined through a pink skin covered by sparse down.

> *The wing is a forelimb and an adaptation to flight that is unique to class Aves. The bones of the hand shows a distinctly different adaptation in birds. The metacarpal bones are fused and taper off into one bone,... the bird-wing 'hand' cannot be moved up and down but has lateral rotation for wing beating.*

How strong wings must be to hold the bird-body in the air no matter what stunts are in process or how full she is of water, insects, seeds or carrion. Birds' flight has always caused envy in humans Birds fly into the unknown, crossing distances that defeat us. It is love and observation of actual birds that leap out of works written long ago, mystic explanations of the human condition in holy allegories like Ibn Sina's *Treatise of the Bird*, which imagines a bird flying up to its original home, as though it were the human soul.

Chaucer borrowed the vision of order and harmony in the community of birds that radiates from earlier Middle Eastern poets, the greatest and most influential being Farid Ud-Din 'Attar's *The Conference of the Birds*, *Mantiq al-tayr*.

Al attar

The birds, the ordinary birds, rare birds, aggressive raucous birds, and shy birds convene because all nations have a ruler, but there is no king for the birds. They feel this lack deeply.

The hoopoe, whose markings show she already knows a thing or two, tells them the right king for them lives far off in a valley beyond the mountains, and his name is Si-murgh, the Griffin. This is the Just Ruler, recurring figure throughout Arab and Muslim cultures. 'He is close to us but we are far from him,' she says.

Excited, the birds plan how to ask him to become their ruler. They argue many points, but it comes down to one thing: who will journey to him? The hoopoe offers to go, but not alone. Many of them, the falcon, the nightingale, the duck, the partridge explains why they would not be able to, actually, on the day. Thousands do set out, but of all those, only thirty make it through the seven long valleys.

There they are made to realise that they themselves are the Si-murgh. The Logic of the symbolism of flight: 'simurgh' means both 30 birds and quest for the first manifestation of the Absolute. It is the flight, the words, the isthmus, the *barzakh*, between the created and uncreated orders.

'Attar, the thirteenth century Persian pharmacist who wrote the book, has wedded birds, Persian literature and a Sufism representing love. One writer comments that 'Attar "traversed the seven cities of love; but we are still left at the bend of the first street."

The story, the origin of many others, is of course an example of pathetic fallacy, since birds can do little more than fly or bluff in danger, but Okri may be thinking of 'Attar when he writes of the eternal human quest for justice: "a people cannot live without it, and in due course they will be prepared to die to make it possible for their children. *Fables are made of this.*" In Islam, the symbolism of flight is very important.

The Just King's time will be, as the Indonesian poet Ranggawarsita put it, when "the little people can laugh," *wong cilik bisa gumuyu.*

The raised wing of any bird, glimpsed from below is almost naked. The bones are outlined through a pink skin covered by sparse down.

Team Brainstorms Bird Feature

Research first. I'm out there. Filming actual birds.

Need love interest. Make it some big meeting, Big Day Out, or Woodford or something. Valentine's Day, that's it. And Mother Nature, no, hey! Make that Venus, the love-goddess supervises while each of them chooses the mate for this year.

Birds actually often mate for life.

Yeah, well, so they'll be out there in that venue, beautiful day, trees full of birds. Actually, make that a stadium, with all the eagles and hawks and whatever up the top, the smaller ones eating insects and stuff in the middle, and all the seed-eaters, your flocks of pretty parrots and all that down the bottom where we can get a good shot of them. That's a great idea! Every bird in Australia!

Then Venus, who's like maybe Nicole, has one lovely girl-bird, something really bright, no, I know, some sort of little eagle, it'll be sitting on her hand all shy. And three different boy-eagles want her.

All right. Then what about this? All the birds get to vote on which one she should choose, so they say a bit about the rivals. The camera can just pan in on one of each type singing, or quacking or whatever they do, their opinion, and that way kids get to study them a bit. Venus says it's up to the girl-bird but the she's too shy to choose in front of all that crowd.

And wait! At the end, you show all the birds and their mates out on the oval, and they're all doing those courtship rituals, you know, people love all that, winding their necks round each other, strutting their bum-feathers in the air. Oh and lyrebirds, can't leave them out. And maybe some funny music for the waterbirds, like the ducks' waddle and stuff. Then there's a huge fly-past round Venus, Nicole, *no* I've got it, Marcia Hines, perfect my friend! And they all stream away across the sky with maybe some Wagner for the eagles.

The Muslim sages often went back to Plato's discussion in *Phaedrus* of the wing as the most qualified and eminent symbol for the movement of Spirit, as Chaucer married Al 'Attar's *Conference* with his own love of birds to write the Parliament of Fowls. In many traditions at many times flying is associated with freedom from the prison of the body.

Lamarck:

Professor of "Insects & Worms" at Museum of Natural History in Paris. His *Zoological History* propounded evolution in the form of willpower exercised by animals, thereby adapting to their living conditions. Strengthen some organs by use, weaken others by non-use, pass on these traits to offspring. Living organisms change because they want to. You are alive, ergo want to be more alive. You want additional uses for your organs, additional habits. You get them because you want them badly enough to keep trying until they come. L. is loved by progressives and social reformers because his theory suggests perfectibility of humanity.

Darwin, by contrast, attributed evolution not to inheritance of acquired characteristics but to random genetic mutation + survival of those mutations better fitted to their environment = Natural Selection. Mankind and other animal species were not created separately by God but evolved from a common ancestor, probably, he speculated, a bisexual mollusc with a vertebra but no head.

Alfred Hitchcock and the birds The other side of the creek, where the neighbours' grow canola or barley, cockatoos shriek and scream in and out of their roosts in the dead trees, huge unbalanced flocks, whose droppings and discarded feathers foul the vegetation across the banks. It's horrible racket even at this distance. They don't come up here much, except when the calitrus seed-cones are ripe when they come in pairs, small flocks, at most a dozen, like the old days before the paddocks and crops.

Nit comes from mutual cockatoo/galah/human watch. The flock begins to descend, one bird separates from the wheeling crowd and perches on a high point while the others descend to feed, on the ground, on the crop. The guard watches, systematically swivelling its head, cocking an eye up, the other down, this way and that in every direction If it screams in alarm all take flight instantly, vertical lift.

This is keeping nit. Either Aboriginal people pointed it out, or Europeans quickly noticed and recognised their own practice of keeping a reliable but unimportant person in the doorway or along the street, who'd whistle if police or rivals come round the corner, giving the punters at the SP bookie's, the two-up game, sly grog shop, a fighting chance to escape.

In town there'd been a bird I never saw but heard each evening saying "Oh my Gawd," "Oh my Gawd," in an old, old parroty voice from the back verandah as I walked past. Why was I thinking about keeping nit?

Spix's Macaws are brilliant blue parrots once common along wooded creeks of Argentina. Why Spix you ask? Johann Baptiste von Spix identified it for European taxonomy in 1819. Since then their habitat has been steadily destroyed by grazing animals and agriculuture to the point where, by 1990, Spix statistics were: Wild:1. Captivity: 12.

The Permanent Committee for the Recovery of Spix's Macaw was set up.

Therewith a wind, scarcely stirring,

The holders of the captive 12 were persuaded to part with 5. Antonio de Dios, millionaire industrialist in the Philippines, owned most. The lone survivor in the wild was intensely studied for how to behave in the wild, to teach macaws released in the future how to deal with predators, drought, and trappers (who put lime on branches), to the land and.... Holding on like the farm people of Curacao do, he's a symbol to them of surviving in great hardship.

The Committee decided to free a female. She liked and followed the survivor, but he wasn't apparently keen to be in a relationship, and soon she was found dead. She'd flown into powerlines. It wasn't really the wilderness that killed her. What makes them think the survivor behaves like macaws used to? Why would it appreciate a mate or a community any more? It is still there, flying, calling, feeding by itself,

2002 Macaw Statistics: Wild: 1.
           Captivity: 61.

~//~

A garden saw I full of blossomy boughs
On every branch the birds heard I sing,
With voice of angel in their harmony;

145

some beside them hear the birds forth bring

Of instruments of strings in tune
Heard I so play a ravishing sweetness,
That God, that maker is of all and Lord,
Never heard better, as I guess.
Therewith a wind, scarcely stirring,
Made in the green leaves a noise soft
According to the birds' song.

This was on Saint Valentine's day
When every fowl cometh there to choose his mate,
Of every kind you could think,
And that so huge noise gan they make that earth,
And air and tree and every lake
So full was, there was scarcely space
For me to stand, so full was all the place.

*As a bird approaches for landing, it must slow down, and it does
so by rotating its wings to a steeper angle. This rotation stops the
smooth flow of air over the wings' surface and causes turbulence.
Turbulence would stall the flying bird and cause it to drop to the
ground rather than skilfully alighting on a branch. The alula pre-
vents this from happening. By raising the first finger and so raising
the alula at the same time, the bird opens up a slot between the
main part of the wing and the alula on the front edge of the wing.*

Sources Include

Geoffrey Chaucer, *Parlement of Foules* (1478): 'A garden saw I...';
'Most avian species...', 173; 'A small songbird...', 9; 'Feathers of
wing...,' 'The wing is a forelimb...', 8; 'As a bird approaches..,' 22.

Gisela and Lesley Kaplan, J. Rogers, *Birds: their Habits and Skills*
(Crows Nest, NSW: Allen & Unwin, 2001).

Farid Ud-Din 'Attar, *The Conference of the Birds*, trans. Mantiq Ut-
Tair (London: Routledge & Kegan Paul, 1954).

Ben Okri, *A Way of Being Free* (Phoenix, Mass.: Market Paperback
1998) 108.

MARTIN HARRISON

BRONZEWINGS WITH LIGHTNING

The bronzewings
pick their way through,
fossicking in pre-storm stillness
jabbing at the car tracks, drilling the dirt
under trees—

choosing such silence—
windlessness like flat sea—

napes as blue-grey as the horizon,
their faces that striped flash
which might happen anytime now,

in the lull, in the air's gap,
pecking
then motionless,
camouflaged by the grass,
merging half-noticed
in tumbled bark's dry litter, dead leaves,

until they're disturbed,
not worried enough to take flight
(an edge of the mind issue),
still walking
with an irritable glance and
mechanical jutting neck
as if someone's pulling puppet strings
through backbone and breast structure:

they pause, then make off
into further, deeper
middle distance, a farness
which stretches westerly under trees,
across half-cleared paddocks, wispy slopes
where dry declivities become watercourses,
under hillsides scarred with rocks—

again to rummage nervously, then freezing,
making sure they're not seen
(indistinct, earth-coloured rubble),
and when they are seen
drawing attention, like children,
to their own mimicking stillness,

such being the quiet which lets them melt
into pale straw, grey stone, fallen timber,
inexpressibly at home in tree-scattered country,
country with no edges,
some nameless slope

stretched with broken, rusty fences—
a delicate, traipsed through, low grade patch
in need of losing its melancholy,
in need of
being restored, re-thought, re-lived—

the two bronzewings are voyagers here
hurtling through time,
held in mind for a second
under the sky's bowl

both now evaporated into
the grass and leaves

yes, two of them

*

Things. Marks in the ground. Things bare stony ground. It's what the machine's whirring sound seems like—a bare place with stones, pebbles, small hand-sized rocks. Car noise, plane noise. In fact, planes pass over so far up that they hang inside their own envelope of silence, like white tubes passing across a soundless screen. Sometimes you glimpse the triangular tail-fin, a flash of blue or red—

Striations. Marks in the ground. Pock marks in stone—weather spots, rain crevices. Not the same as the broad marks which late light is throwing as streaks across dead grass: groves, stone-rot, revelations of sedimentary lines

Each mark has its own mind, its own reason for being. Each of them lock into invisible structures of word and thought—utterances, humming, stray thoughts, learnt thoughts...that thing I meant to say

that thing which could be sad

Gaps, in a sense. Though there are no gaps. Closeness, though there is no distance. A full, perfect moment: but some would call it empty.
(two people not aware that they love each other)

(the sky god saturated in blue)

(two people attuned to each other)

(the give and take of love making)

(my body immersed in you)

This thought between things

*

until the thunder comes back, after a five minute rainstorm seemed to have ended the matter. The birds had gone by under the trees half an hour ago, almost as if in another world. A few minutes after, we ran back to the house, even though the clouds, becoming a single thunderhead, ever fully darkened the air. The storm fell in diamond strings, fleshed with light, and then in long scattered drops, darting by in a pattern of flashes and strips. Enough rain to soak the tin, but not much more. Lightning had come through, moved on, as it if was wandering the country, scavenging, looking things out. The air hardly cooled: it stayed thick as a thermal blanket. Pale shadows clustering on branches, down the sides of tree trunks

dull thunder noise:
it ripples somewhere—
northwards.

*

Later, too, intense whitening heat would be over for a few hours, a
cool interlude lasting through the night, cooling things down, cooling
the touch of wood and earth, cooling our bodies, cooling our touch,
cooling caves and crevices. Everyone hopes this is what our night is
like. Didn't you feel the space then, right then, like the edge of an
imaginary darkness? Didn't you wonder at the trailings of steps and
voices: across time, yes, but more across your mind. Across you, across
the glimpse opening up in you.

Did you remember how absorbed we were, lost in the birds as if we
could drown in the blended dust and leaves

bronzewings, dancing, fluttering up, through the glare

dust and twigs formed, perfect, like a hearth

you leaning forward, thoughtful, beautiful
while, momentarily, cicadas start up their wave-banks of sound like
an enormous drawn-out breath, one breath after the other lapping,
overlapping, linking, one with another. And right in the middle of the
aquamarine sky-clearing which the rain burst has made, an instant
reminder: overhead, a last thud, laughing, inside a timber house knocks
a chair over on to the wooden floor with a cracking sound we can hear
from outside   Yes, like a grenade exploding, a single thunder burst,
high up, smacks the sky

ERIC ROLLS

PLACES THAT
MATTER TO ME

Places that matter to me—well what matters more than my first farm? It sloped from a low hill in a neighbour's property across a black-soil plain, down to dark chocolate self-mulching flats on the Namoi River in the north-west of New South Wales. Self-mulching soils loosen themselves as they dry out. When wet they are sticky, and as intractable as molasses; when dry they are as fluffy as eiderdown. The top six centimetres can be raked through the fingers. If a drop of water falls on the surface, one or two crumbs absorb it immediately. They swell. Multiply the drop by a shower of rain. The whole surface of the ground swells. It rises to meet the rain. If the shower persists, the lower crumbs lift the surface in tiny bumps. The ground rolls about, rejoicing in the rain.

The Namoi was then a living river. It threaded the farm with life: fish, birds, trees. Plants grew out of the river and climbed the bank; plants grew down the bank into the water. It was a marvel to take up a handful of soil and realise it was my responsibility. If I treated it well it would treat me well.

It gave me experiences that I could never hope for. It displayed them once in a lifetime.

One early morning I was down by the river and I watched a triangle of hares. Hares are not native; they were first brought to Victoria in 1859 as game and for coursing with greyhounds. At first they bred up quickly and damaged gardens and fruit trees. For several years they were about in thousands, then the numbers settled down. We had seven or eight living permanently on our farm of about 450 hectares.

The triangle consisted of an old buck, an old doe, and a young doe with shining hair and the full rounded body of the three-quarter grown.

I don't think she had ever been mated with, and the buck was chasing her about amongst new-sprung grass in a clump of bimble boxes. She would stand and let the buck approach. He would smell her and stroke her back with his paws, but just as he would clasp her and go to mount, she would buck him off and canter away.

The old doe was furious. She longed for the buck and kept running in front of him and propping with her haunches raised ready for him. He either side-stepped her or leaped over her as though she were a log in his way. Four times she so presented herself in vain, and when he skipped round her the fifth time she stood up, reached out with her forepaws and boxed him on the ears, one, two, with audible smacks. The young doe stopped and turned round to see what the noise was. The buck approached her vigorously. He thumped the ground with a hind shank and leaped upon her. She relaxed and seemed for a moment to welcome him, then she sprang, twisted, and kicked him a metre away on to his back, then ran hard towards long grass on the river bank. The buck sat up and scratched a boxed ear and the old doe made off slowly, sometimes looking back to see if the buck would follow. He didn't.

When tractor driving at night one is enclosed with one's machinery in a sphere of light. The black wall of night recedes before the tractor and closes in again behind the plough. Usually nothing is revealed but the changeless furrow. One night a fat-tailed sminthopsis ran in front of the tractor. She was lumpy and odd-looking with seven young ones clinging to the fur on her back and sides. They are pretty creatures, about the size of a house mouse, patterned in grey and white. The wide tail stores fat to tide them over lean times. She jumped down into the furrow then out on to the worked ground and headed for the darkness. As she sprang out of the furrow one of the young ones fell off. I stopped the tractor and picked it up. It squeaked. The mother heard and ran back to claim it. I held my hand with the young one in it close to the ground. She stopped a few centimetres away, chattered a little, then hopped up into my palm. The young one scrambled on to her back again and she turned and ran for the comforting darkness.

I still remember the next story with delight, especially as I wrote it for the old *Bulletin*'s column called 'Aboriginalities'. It was the first piece of nature writing I had ever done. It, too, happened late one night as I drove a tractor. A leveret ran ahead of me in the furrow. It seemed to be running very fast, but since the tractor was travelling at only seven kilometres an hour, it was short legs that made it seem so; it was no more than a day or two old. Bewildered by the light and the noise, it was unwilling to leave the furrow even though I slowed down several times. It was a good, unobstructed path to run in. When it was obviously tiring, I stopped the tractor and got off to pick it up and move it. As I approached, it ran into the protection of the deep shadow under the front tractor wheel and flattened itself between tyre and ground. I picked it up by the loose skin at the back of the neck. It cried out sharply and astonishingly loudly for such a small animal. At once there was a heavy thumping not far away in the darkness. It frightened me. It sounded like a big animal and there should have been no big animals in the paddock. The baby hare cried out again. It was answered by more thumping, then the sound of something running towards me. Whatever it was out there was charging.

Into the circle of light came the mother hare. She ran on her front legs, stepped high with her back legs and drummed the full length of the shank on the ground with every step. The noise was as loud as a galloping horse. She ran right up to me and smelled at the young one in my hand. It cried out again. The mother leaped in the air, thudded both shanks on the ground, then stood up, held out her fore paws for balance and worked her hind legs alternately in a frenzied tattoo that increased in speed and loudness. Her legs blurred. No jazz drummer ever moved his sticks so fast.

I released her baby. She stopped, dropped on to four feet, leant forward and wrinkled her nose over it, licked it a few times, then led it off quietly into the night.

Hares are known to dance together. In the early morning a couple stand on a mound, touch fore paws, then kick out their long hind legs in unison. That is something I still hope to see.

When Elaine and I were packing to leave Cumberdeen, my last farm, a very old hare came to live in the garden. He had been in many a fight because his ears were torn and there were old scars on his belly from scratches. He was thin and weak. He had come to the good food in the garden where he would be safe from predators in his last few days, but he seemed to need some final company. As we moved around, we would look up and see him sitting quietly in the shade where he could see one of us.

In the late afternoon when we sat on the verandah with a glass of wine, our hare came to sit quietly on the other side of the floor-to-ceiling gauze wall. When we talked to him he turned to look in through the gauze. Then one evening he wasn't there. I like to think that he died peacefully somewhere in the long grass instead of being torn to pieces by a wedge-tailed eagle or a fox.

CHARLIE WARD

TERRITORY DIRGE

Oxidised desert iron, bleached of ages bled by air
Red dunes folded, endless sea of shifting cloth
falling rising, sandy waves rising falling,
blue beneath moon and glowing strident under sun,
a sea sandily crossing a continent, ten inches a year

Gibber roasted iron ingot-vegies,
blackbright baking trays, one inch deep ten miles across
earth and air face off—meteor spray lies gibber-mixed
Wild camels gently press fallen stars under padded feet
Owls move silent by the night and sleep slow,
guarding mulga clumps by day
claws clasping wood so hard you burn it green

Papunya Uluru Hermannsberg
Cats bred khaki hid better than dingoes
like raven, too smart for roadkill, too quick for traps
Two feet knee-high, finches king-hit dead,
before bore trough take- off, no last cry
Feral feasting birdblood garnet red today
delicious indelicate dissection under acacia chandeliers,
waving gentle feather wisps in endless easy breeze

Sediment sandworn, eon ground dissolving cloak
dust rolling skyward, eastward, westward, just away
Ground glowing purple shares hues of air in desert dusk
coming after days of hunting time.

Empty-plained illusion betrayed by
smoky towers that loom and teeter,
giving away old Holdens with open doors,
sweaty barrel chested fire farmers in greasy flannel
clutch burning torches,
throw spinifex fire fronts
greasy black resin cloud columns rise
high through perfect air

Legless lizards and marsupial moles bound
slithering from dark dusty tunnels hidden in
needle-stack sap clumps littering the plains
Clustered wedgetails play between fire and sky,
soaring, seeking, swooping prey before firestick farmers below

Fregon Mutijulu Amata
In the Tanami, the flat abounds with termite towers
infinitesimal earthly astronomers living underground,
in African mud hut observatories,
scattered with the random certainty of casual constellations
moorish mound sentinels tracing lost myths,
tracking celestial hoboes down the milky star river of night
Mind scorched silent, lost in dreamless purgatorial siestas
    by day,
these termitaries the marooned queens from a giant chess set,
deserted on the road to Damascus, or maybe rabbit flat

Arapunya Narwietooma Barrow Creek Nyrripi
Washouts meandering, arroyos carved in earthchurning
    downpours,
come up rarer than fire, darker than dust storms
Creek banks chalky dry dust, lays earth-scalpelled open
Dirt banks studded by river rocks dropped from glaciers
grinding through worlds gone by

Switchback creeks trace lightning routes jagged as torn paper
Lazy places saving lizard tracks from drifting winds until
    some
crazy storm blows up, punching the breakaways
Staccato electro-static thunderclaps bringing cloudbursts in
    tow,
Water dumped down narrow channels
—the language of life for eyes come later in further desert days
Eggs and seeds as hard as rocks tuned for the raindrop
    moment,
for invisible petal dust to germinate flowers,
soaking open the bubblesacs of buddhamind frogs,
the wet wakeup call for desert crabs who didn't think to leave
when the seas dried up and seaweed blew away

Dagaragu Pigeon Hole Kalkaringi Timber Creek
Forest country, flat country, meeting country, Mataranka
    country
Roads from savannah and south and saltwater country
top end gateway, dustblown sitdown, greencan camp or
    jurassic spring.
Artesian water flows free and clear as beer
weird water bubbles into prehistoric swampland
crystal, mineral-tang
cuts glowing passages through dinosaur country
Thread-thin algae bathes in clear metal canals
as lazy sulphorous silver bubbles float free,
popping, surface-topping another dinosaur day

Parchment paperbarks,
swimming through the wet, pale on blackbark, burning up
    the dry.
When fires come, old lettery layers smoke,
smouldering shrouds clinging to the shanks of stick-figure
    ghosts
paperbark forest men wrapped in white,
flaky decay belying deep dug roots dark-mudded below
melaleuca cracked earth offers orchids and lily bulbs when
    wet water time breaks
and sweet rain washes through the trees
patient frogs sing up sweaty downpours,
raising rain to the height of treeknees
Waders on twigscroll raft nests paddle between paperbarks
    with eggshell oars

Borroloola Ngukkurr Numbulwar Nhulunbuy
Sweetwater billabongs teem with two winged traffic,
egret pairs stand stilted silently,
waiting for fish beneath the beating wings of banded ducks,
airborne friars in black collar mourning,
harbingers of soft-mud-secrets dreaming,
long-legged navigators dancing two-step in stilted duets

Buffaloes mob, rush and wallow the plains,
roaming free spirits, released from eternities of rice-paddy
    servitude.
Big, black, scythe-sharp sights giving glimpses of Asia

thunder-footed immigrants, revelling in the wide ranging
    freedom of no-stop-sign plains,
letting black mud wallows and knock'em down winds absorb
    all care, all memories of home.

On the edge of the buffalo run, plains twisted thick with
    billygoat plum,
long yam vines curling overhead adjoin
screw palms clumped for frogs thronging dusk recitals.
Bush too thick for a dog to bark, crunch- leaf carpet
flung over undulating floor clinging to the base of basalt
    skirting boards

Gove Gunbalunya Murgenella
Ramingining ragged-cliffs roll mile-on-mile,
boulder jumbles glued with elastic fig roots,
roughleaved ficus push for anchorage,
pulling green livelihood from deep private places.
Twisting ledges, granite chip mazes,
honeycombs hide those that sleep, and dream, and oversee
    the land.
Wallabies in dusty nests,
cocooned crack-clinging goannas,
toast their toes in fireball lightfall.
moons too, pass rays glancing through dark crack doorways
Old people ochre bone- wrapped,
protectors of country, of memories, protected in turn.

Numbulwar Wadeye Mandorah Maningrida
Saltwater sea eagle soars, softly searching empty beaches,
silent witness of boulder-rolling crab-creepers
stem-eyed sidesteppers making
muddy marbles between tides
industrious idiots

In flat country, sandy tidal salty country,
mud-colour riversnakes coil, lolling, seaward bound
six metre moon magic playing push me pull me
through serpentine mangrove corridors.
Raptor's dinner a coiling dead sea snake
smelling languid, hollow crab claws filled with mud.

LAURIE KUTCHINS

WATERMARK QUILT

(A Found Poem, based on voices gathered for the Watermark
Muster, Laurieton NSW, October 2003).

> Under the tin roof of the boathouse
> > the clap sticks call the rain down
> > > and the rain calls three black cockatoos back
> > > to nest.

> > Let us become the bell.

> > > * * *

> I belong to a place with the random optimism of a million
> spiders.
> > I belong to a place where messiness works,
> > > every bug with its grace and purpose.

> > > * * *

> The country is singing to me. sing it up,
> > > but does the place really hear me?

> Does the land get unhealthy because it is not sung?

> I tell it, it is beautiful, like an old woman
> who hasn't been told that for awhile.
> > > But does it hear me?

> I know that if I sing the rock pool up
> > from the face of the deep,
> > > the crabs are more healthy.

> > > * * *

> This place is what I know as the place gives way to changes
> > I cannot stop.

The change is like a one-eyed giant
I cannot get around.
        I need to stand here.
            I need to make the giant
            blink,

and see the little leaf that has been shaking with my heart.

* * *

I could never own that grassland. I belong to it.

I come home from the ocean hungry for earth,
        a line of hills
            I might be imagining.

My totem is the brown snake.

I know the small gray mangrove heron knows more
                about the estuary
                    than I know.

* * *

The place I am married to is a landscape that is dominated
    by water.

The place I am having a love affair with is a place filled
        with charismatic animals and deeply embedded voices,
            with macropods thumping by the tent at night,
                with the wide swath of python tracks
                across the path,
                    with a brown snake
                        I have yet to meet.

As a newcomer, how will I serve the places I fall in love with?

* * *

I belong to the life cycle of grasses. The bush is not silence.

When I go back to those mountains, something cracks open
  in me.
        Like its light, and its air, and its stones,
                        I am different there.

The road is every bit as important as the arrival.

    Sometimes the place is large, sometimes very small.

        I should have stayed where everything is grass.

                    * * *

The rumblings of the heavy trucks we hear on the road
  outside the hall
      are the logging trucks coming and going
            from our mountain.

                    I met eyes with the loggers this morning
                    on the road.

The rocks are training us.
        The stones are finding their way downriver.

Sometimes I go back there and see it is all I have ever known.
      Sometimes I go back
            and find I don't know it.
I could not find a song about evaporation.

                    We don't want Sorry—
                    we only want to be acknowledged.

                    * * *

My bay is shaped like a womb, there is no sea grass anymore,
      the iridescent peacock colours are gone.
            At times I think of leaving it now, but part of me
                wants to stay and fight it out.

The frigate bird makes me think of my father. He's telling me
      the names of places in the sea
            that I can't make out.

If we could only re-organize ourselves a little.

Heron, tree fern, cello all the same thing.

* * *

I love the tall gum trees swaying in the breeze, I love digging
    a hole
            in the ground to cook,
                    and then back-filling it to undo it.
        When the rains come the grass will grow over the
        backfill.

Who could have invented a platypus?

The dog extends our senses farther out into the world.

The river runs backwards when they turn the pumps on.

* * *

I go to a place with a rocky lookout where I can stand
                            and be in five worlds at
                            once.

I want to understand the verb acknowledge.

Have we made a place for silence?

Listen: this is what the earth requires.

* * *

Stand here. Water has memory.

Stand here. The river is so sad.

We are remembering water has memory.

Stand here

in green verb releasing everything.

LIANA JOY CHRISTENSEN

SLOW STORY MANIFESTO

If arts/humanities are a very poor cousin to science/economics, where does that leave nature writing? What kind of pallid offspring of Victorian gentility and Darwinism is that? Nature writing's lacklustre public image undoubtedly benefited from the late 20th century upsurgence of interest in all things environmental. Ecocriticism constituted itself as a field of study, and debates emerged about the boundaries, nature and function of nature writing. Yet I detect an undercurrent of defensiveness in much of this. Mixed in with many other motivations is the understandable desire to rehabilitate the terminally geeky.

I think it is a mistake, however, to stay on the surface of our cultural stories, and mark out territories for the newly-cool. Nature writing is *this*, it's not *that*. Fiction *does/does not* count. Nature writing *should be/should not be* overtly political, scientific, poetic. An entire critical industry could be erected on the basis of such debates. Yet they are, in essence, the replication of worn-out power struggles. It is the triumph of style over substance. Oh by all means, let us have debates. Let them be raging and glorious. But let them lead to depth, diversity and opening, not boundary-policing and closure.

At the *Watermark* gathering in October 2003 I floated the notion of a slow story movement, analogous to the slow food movement. I believe the connections among nature, sustenance and story are more subtle and inseparable than we think. Story—like water, air and food—is essential for survival. Viktor Frankl,[1] writing as a Holocaust survivor, furnished good evidence that, *in extremis,* the stories people told themselves about their values and their futures were often a better predictor of survival than other, more physical factors. The stories we tell about the world are directly connected to our actions and non-actions in the world. Many of us now recognise we are in the middle of a holocaust against nature, in which humans and humanity are 'collateral damage'. This holocaust results from the big stories we have told about the nature of nature, and the nature of humanity. We can't change what follows from those narratives simply by rearranging the surface features of the story so that it is more EC (ecologically correct). That is merely decorating the status quo with greenery. We need to understand and rework the root stories if we wish to end up with different, more sustainable ways of being in the world.

Our entire conceptual universe is composed of stories. We have political stories, scientific stories and economic stories. Some stories accrue power; others are overshadowed. We miss our greatest opportunities if we fail to comprehend the latent power that resides in being creators, tellers, lovers of story. Why not go deep-diving into cultural stories, and come up with strange luminous fish? Why not change the weather by shifting the currents at depth, slowly? Why not laugh at what is most painful? Why not get good and angry? That is the real challenge for nature writers.

My personal taxonomy of stories runs thus: toxic stories, junk food stories, sustaining stories. All manifest at both the individual and the cultural level. Fundamentalism, for instance, is a toxic story writ large. Junk food stories are pacifiers, disconnected from moral or political action: the rescued-kitten-segment on the non-news; reality TV. Toxic stories are pernicious and persistent, but perhaps easier to recognise as dangerous. Toxic stories can poison slowly, or in an instant. Junk food stories, like junk food itself, are rarely fatal in a single dose. Low-level intake is even justifiable. But at length, a wholesale diet of junk for the body/mind *fails to sustain*.

We all suffer some degree of poisoning from toxic stories, both cultural and personal. We are all malnourished. Stories will sustain us, only if we sustain them. The slow story is the sustaining one. The slow story is never simply yours alone—it is always in connection. In other words, it is both deeply personal and also transpersonal. To truly honour slow stories is the work of a lifetime. They are nourished in silence, in suffering, as well as in joy and celebration. They will always move beyond you to the world.

The fruit of the slow story movement will be bountiful and not readily classified by current measures. Each text eclectic, the whole body eclectic: bound to confound the cataloguers, perplex the publishers. They already inhabit odd shelves, waiting for the serendipitous browser to trail through libraries and bookshops. Sometimes sonorous and sometimes grating, these echoes of a slow, tectonic shifting in worldview will in time create a sustaining symphony. Joyous proof that music is made through silence, discord, difference, moving in and out of harmony.

You doubt?

For good reason, most of us have become deeply suspicious of big stories. Yet, that suspicion has in no way prevented toxic big stories from waxing fat. It is as if the kings recognised they were about to be held accountable for all they had wrought on the bodies of women, of people of colour, of working class men, of the earth itself. By the end of the century of wars, the big stories of Christianity, science and communism could no longer be adhered to blindly and proudly. So the kings abdicated, but before departing they burned the crops and salted the soil. The creators of a ruined land, they now take a perverse pride in the failure of their utopian projects. Disbarring the possibility of more inclusive, more sustaining big stories created by the others they feared, they have now converted their position to one of domination in absentia. They have reckoned without the power of that which has always been beneath their notice. They sit in exile from the world, celebrating cynicism, valorising dystopias, mocking the big stories of others. Yet all the while the overlooked—the women, the weeds, the under-kingdom of invertebrate—continue to do their slow, partial work of reclamation.

We need the big picture to recognise that bride-burning and foot-binding and anorexia/bulimia and silicon toxicity are not unrelated accidents of completely relative cultural histories. And to understand that gender politics cannot be disconnected from deforestation, Chernobyl, the enhanced greenhouse effect and salination to offer just a small sample of our ecological woes. Big sustaining stories can be created without falling under the seductive spell of the seamless stories of the past. They can be patch-worked from diverse *petit recits*, little stories; robust, hybrid, created as a way of connecting to and giving meaning to a life lived in a particular place and time. If some are sharp and political, others will be lovingly lyrical. Their wildness will be domestic, far from grand. They will look at length and deeply into what is at hand. The world will only sustain us if we sustain the world. Like people, the world needs to be really seen, touched and loved in order for it to thrive. Not just intellectually, but physically and spiritually. Often indigenous people are much clearer about these responsibilities—but the task in great and all hands are needed here. The work may sometimes happen quickly, but it can never be hurried. It demands depth and presence. This is work worth the doing. This is a slow story manifesto.

Notes

1   Viktor E. Frankl, *Man's Search for Meaning* (1946, trans 1963; rev. and updated, New York: Washington Square Press, 1984).

NICK DRAYSON

SEEING THINGS

Look up. There they are—fast black shapes scything the blue. No, not the swallows, flitting and fluttering on delicate wings. Up higher. The swifts. The swifts have arrived.

Was there ever a bird named better? Swifts do not fly; they speed. 100 kph?—just cruising. Fifty swifts at least are cruising the wind above me, soaring and swooping on sickle wings. I can see they are of two kinds. Large dark ones with a white band front and back and blunt tail—needletails. And slightly smaller ones with white throats and sharp black tails. When one swerves in a fast turn its tail fans into a V—fork-tailed swifts. Each bird a drawn bow, fast and silent, no labour in its perfect movement.

I delight in seeing swifts—for their beauty, and because on a hot summer's day they mean that a change is on the way. Swifts are nomads; their home is the sky. All day they ride the winds ahead of a front or around a storm, feeding on flying insects. At night they rest. Needletails land wherever the wind has taken them, clinging to the bark of a tree or a high rock (though their claws are sharp, it is the needle-like projections from the ends of their tail feathers that has given them their name). Forktailed swifts do things differently. From the day they leave their parents' nest to the day they make their own, they are always on the wing. For two years, perhaps more, they touch neither ground, nor tree, nor rock. Each night, and sometimes by day, forktailed swifts will fly high up into the air, perhaps rising thousands of metres if they find a big thermal. Then they circle slowly down. If they sleep, they sleep in flight.

Neither kind of swift breeds in Australia. They come in late spring, feed on our summer crop of flying insects, and in March or April head back across the equator to their breeding grounds in northern Asia. Any insect that fits into a swift's mouth is food, but when that short black beak is open it's a big mouth, stretching wide across the head. To drink, the birds swoop low over pond or creek and scoop up water as they fly. I like swifts. They are wondrous birds.

Now, look down. Do you see that ant, pulling the seed along? Don't worry, it won't bite or sting you. It isn't a huge and fearsome bull ant (I've been stung by those more than once and I know how much it hurts—bad as a bee or a wasp I reckon). No, it's just a little black ant— what, two millimetres long? It's hard to put a number on such smallness, but it looks only about half the size of your usual kitchen or garden ant. And it's hard to say how much bigger than the ant is the seed that it's dragging back to its nest. Ten times, twenty? Too big for the little insect to lift, but it's pulling the seed along just fine, over the twigs and rocks. A wattle seed, wouldn't you say? Flat and oval and shiny black, and if you get down close you can see that the ant is tugging the seed along by the little stalk that wattle seeds seem so often to have. Every so often a fellow ant passes by and there's a bit of antennae waving, but the others don't try to help. Only a few centimetres to go now. The little ant will make it to the nest all right.

The entrance to the nest is an irregular hole beside the garden path. Ants are coming and going all the time. One ant comes out carrying a grain of soil—or should that be a rock? It is as big as the insect's head. The ant carries its load a couple of centimetres, drops it and returns to the nest. The entrance to the nest is strewn with not only soil. There are wattle-seeds as well, and some smaller black seeds that look, to this occasional gardener, as though they may have come from the columbines that are growing beside the front door—or do I mean campanulas? "Granny's bonnets". I see another rock emerge, a positive boulder this time, and it is carried by a different kind of ant. Its body must be twice the size of the little one, but its head is enormous, out of all proportion, and with a pair of jaws to match. A soldier ant no doubt, born and bred to defend the nest. Those big jaws would have no trouble with an invader, and seem to have no trouble gripping the boulder, though the soldier does seem to have a problem getting it to fit through the hole. It tries one way, it tries another. At last it manoeuvres the rock through the hole, but then seems to change its mind and retreats, still carrying the rock.

The little ant I saw first is still struggling towards the nest with its seed. Where has it come from? It doesn't take me long to find out. The seed has come from a box-leaf wattle, *Acacia buxifolia*, one that we planted by the fence when we came to the house four years ago. The tree has already grown to four metres and bears a fine crop of twisted pods. It is from one of these that the seed has come. I pace out the distance to the nest. Six metres. I know that you can't really compare sizes and distances across such a wide scale, but I do it anyway. Ant, two millimetres; five hundred ants to the metre. So six metres is about three thousand ant lengths. What this little insect has done is equivalent to me dragging a one tonne weight over a five kilometre army assault course.

The big ant is still having problems with its rock. In and out, in and out, and all the time the smaller workers are running past or between its legs. It occurs to me that perhaps I've misunderstood what is happening. Perhaps the big ant is the doorman and the boulder is a door that it is opening and closing. I don't know. The smaller ant arrives with its seed, and both disappear into the darkness of the nest.

But why have so many of the wattle seeds been left outside the nest? I pick one up to compare with one I took from beneath the wattle tree. Same size, same shape, but the one discarded beside the entrance to the nest has something missing. That little white stalk that once held the seed onto the pod is gone. It was this, the aril (I pronounce it like "arid" but some say 'ah-ril'), that the little ant had been gripping as it pulled the seed towards the nest. The aril is the only thing the ants can eat—the seed itself is much to hard even for an ants tough little jaws. But the little worker ant couldn't remove the aril by itself. It had to drag the whole seed back to the nest, where the edible part could be cut off by the powerful mandibles of a soldier.

This ant/wattle arrangement is quite common in Australia. Many of our wattles (with over 700 species of *Acacia*, Australia is wattle capital of the world) have fleshy arils, full of fat and sugar, that are irresistible to ants. And many of our ants don't seem to mind lugging the seeds away to their nests for processing, thus dispersing the seeds away from the tree. Both plant and insect benefit.

As to which species of ant I am watching, I'm afraid I don't know. I know what it isn't. It isn't a bull ant or a jack jumper in the sub-family Myrmeciinae, with powerful stings, long jaws and pugnacious disposition. It isn't a meat ant of the genus *Iridomyrmex*, decorating its low domed nest with small white pebbles and swarming out when the nest is disturbed. Nor is it a shiny nocturnal sugar ant, genus *Camponotus*, with gleaming black head and abdomen. It is one of the other thousand or more species of ant in Australia. Someone once told me that there are more ant species just on Black Mountain in Canberra than in the whole of the British Isles (while I am sure that this reflects the abundance of ants in Australia, I suspect it may also reflect the fact that the CSIRO Division of Entomology happens to be at the foot of Black Mountain).

The soldier ant appears again, this time without its boulder. It comes straight out of the nest and hurries along the path the smaller ant had taken, but after a few seconds it turns back. Another large-headed soldier appears from the nest, then another, and another, fanning from the hole. Dozens of little workers appear, not carrying anything, just scurrying around in ever increasing numbers. Something is happening.

A different kind of ant appears. Larger than the soldier but with a small head, it begins clambering over seeds and soil and smaller relations with no discrimination. It has wings. One of the soldiers appears to be pushing it back down the hole, but then another winged ant appears. It looks clumsy and aimless, but resists attempts to persuade it to return to the nest. More winged ants appear, and more. The ants are about to swarm.

All summer long the nest has been preparing for this event—those little worker ants bringing food to the nest, the soldier ants guarding it from attack, and deep down underground the queen. She has been laying thousands of eggs, most of which are brought up as sterile workers or soldiers. But some have now been fertilised by the sperm she has stored inside her. These are the ones that are appearing now—the male alates, or flying ants. Even bigger alates are appearing, the females. All around, all over the neighbourhood, the same special coincidence of time and humidity and air pressure is the trigger for other nests to begin swarming. Soon the air will be filled with flying ants.

Up the flying ants will go, higher and higher in their nuptial flight, each female looking for a male, each male looking for a female. They will couple on the wing and fall back to earth. The lucky ones will land near some soft ground and start to dig a new nest, home for a new colony of ants. The unlucky ones? They may not find a mate, or they will find a mate but not a nest site. Or they will be snapped up by birds. Look up. The swifts are flying lower now. You can almost hear the snap of their wide black bills.

COLLEEN Z. BURKE

SPLICING AIR
> Sprung from
> shrivelled down
> dam waters
> lithe
> petrified limbs
> of dead
> gumtrees
> splice air
> tumultuous with
> storm clouds
> and mountains

TURMOIL OF CLOUDS
> Beneath a
> turmoil of clouds
> and storms
> gouged peaks
> of Big Talbingo
> mountain
> crackling
> with electricity
> are lightly
> etched
> with snow
> flakes

AFTER A LONG DROUGHT
> Spring rain
> drumming down
> churned up
> orange soil
> bright amidst
> scraps of green
> and the random
> upsurge
> of grey rocks
> and boulders

DAVID PRATER

SPRING*

   spring wrapped in shrouds feel the desperation
   of my punches in our daydreams*
   speak to us without
   mouths bruised harmonies

   your soft sounds reach but do not enter me yet
   you are a frozen river & i a boat*
   ice-locked & vengeful
   spewing steam

   the moment your word becomes a bird & takes flight
   even rumour turns on like the truth*
   painted on a window
   thunder pines

   spring you are a curl of smoke blown diagonally
   & a forest shot through with vapour trails*
   or bullets that tremble
   sunlight hammers

   a thousand restless revolutions in your wings
   when i sleep a child is born*
   not knowing how to run
   not in my dream

   & you'll come again soon like a rain of stones
   against the doorway of my love*
   ajar but your sweetness &
   light!—I cry out!

BUSTLING

on the streets & the subway
discern the bustle of inane conversations
in the soul food cafe gravy
taste the fried meat flavour bustling
in the park, through the haze
see the bustling squirrels' business
after the parade, on broadway
police bustle—do not cross
in their curt replies, inquiries
ignore the bustling self-obsession
in the evening, this aftermath
fill your houses with bustling activity
at the crossing over, the tide
bustle like you mean it—be bustly

EMPIRES BETWEEN

just as the sand in the zone
where it meets the sea is wet
so too my heart in this terminal
or that economy class reflects
the between-ness of things, the
false empiricism of old bones

see the western world before
somebody blows it up forever
into a ballooning & bloated
donkey's carcass that will never
deflate or cease expanding, on
a course with some crashing bore

cynicism's been rocked by semtex
morphing into the plastic now
of rubble, the beards of surfers
brand new t-shirt cash cows
& the gritty stubble of death
wrapped not in shrouds but syntax

→ → →

WRITER AND READER

→ → →

VERONICA BRADY

Mark Tredinnick (ed), *A Place on Earth: An Anthology of Nature Writing from Australia and North America*. (Lincoln and London, University of Nebraska Press, 2003)

There is an image in Chaucer's Pardoner's Tale which has always haunted me, the old man who walks the earth, "lyk a restetees kaityf", knocking on the ground with his staff crying;

> ...'Leeve mooder, leet me in!
> Lo how I vanysshe, flessh, and blood, and skyn!
> Allas! whan shul my bones been at reste?

And now, reading this collection of nature writing from Australia and North America, it returns to set the context and perhaps also the purpose of my response to these essays. There is and always has been a great deal of writing of this kind in North America but, as Mark Tredinnick points out in his introduction to this collection, there is much less of it in this country than in the USA and Canada. This is probably the result of the differences in our histories, North America being settled when metaphysics were in vogue and land figured in that metaphysical scheme, whereas non-Aboriginal Australia is largely the product of British imperial ambitions in which land was seen as mainly an economic resource.

As a result there is almost something apologetic about much Australian nature writing, as if caring for the natural world and finding it valuable in and for itself were somehow subversive and against the national interest—usually defined in terms of terms of material rather than imaginative productivity. Indeed in the present political climate the concern with the land as the outer equivalent of an inner reality, once central to much of our writing, is no longer in vogue, with Les Murray and in quieter vein Robert Gray and David Malouf almost alone in their sense of what Murray has called a 'deeply reassuring current of sheer meaning... a pressure of significance' to be found in the world beyond the self.

North America, however, is different. Nature writing not only continues to flourish there but to express a confident sense of belonging, of affinity between human beings and the world they live in not to be found in most Australian writing. So for James Galvin, for instance, an island in the river in the Neversummer Mountains, remote and largely untouched by humans, is 'the real world', but also a world in tune with humanity, 'wearing a necklace of waterways, concentrically nested inside the darker green of pines, and then the gray-green of sage and the yellow-green of prairie grass.'

By and large North American writers still seem to hold the Enlightenment's confident belief that human beings can read the Book of Nature and are in fact its primal self-referent. In the snow-clad mountains around him, John Haines, for example, can see a 'text that has been written there for thousands of years'. True, as he continues, 'I was not here, and will not be in winters to come, to read it'. But the point is that he is able to do so now. Unlike Chaucer's old man he does not need to be let into the mystery of the earth. He is already inside it. As Emerson put it, the natural world echoes the inner life of the soul. So these writers then are, as Barry Lopez states, not only 'alert for some "numinous event" in the world about them but often find it there'. In that sense their writing can be seen as religious in the best sense of that shop-soiled word.

In his introduction Tredinnick wonders why things are different in Australia, asking 'what it is about this land of mine, then, that has failed to inspire' this kind of writing. Places do not naturally occur— they are the product of human imagination as well as physical fact—so this is a question to ponder. What is it about the way Australians have imagined place which is different from the North American one? After all we are all products of settler societies, transplanted peoples who were faced with the task of coming to terms with the new landscape in which we found ourselves and writing about nature has always been an important way of doing this. Why have we responded so differently?

Gary Snyder, himself a distinguished nature writer and poet, points out that indigenous peoples are not faced with this task since they have lived so long and closely with nature that their relationship with it is taken for granted, lived rather than talked about. The Australian Tim Winton makes a similar point in his essay in this collection. But he has more to say about indigenous people and this relationship, perhaps because our culture generally is more troubled in our dealings with them than the North Americans seem to be. There is even a long essay here by Linda Hogan, a Chickasaw poet, novelist and essayist which confesses a kind of envy of 'the practical mysticism' of Aboriginal people, quoting the elder Bill Neidjie:

> I love it tree because e love it too.
> E watching me same as you.

In her essay Linda Hogan says something similar, explaining that 'inside the people who grow out of any land there is an understanding of it, a remembering all the way back to origins, to when the gods first shaped humans out of clay, back to when animals could speak with people'. One of the strengths of these essays then lies in the way they respect this view and thus challenge our present sense of reality and value, reminding us that it may well be, as Heidegger argues, 'poetically that we dwell upon earth' and it is

> When thought's courage stems from
> the bidding of Being, then
> destiny's language thrives.
>
> As soon as we have the thing before
> our eyes, and in our hearts an ear
> for the word, then thinking prospers.

But the essays in this anthology make it clear that Australians seem to have found it harder to hear this 'bidding of Being'—or perhaps North Americans feel that it has done their bidding and so can live more easily with it. This is not the place to discuss the historical and cultural reasons for this difference. But as an Australian reader I think it is worth looking at what it tells us about ourselves, which seems to be what most of these essays ask us to do.

To begin with, it appears that most Australian writers here want, as Tredinnick confesses in his introduction, to belong and want to do so 'very deeply'. For him belonging is essential to his identity: 'You cannot know me until you know the weather and the country that surround me, the trees and rocks and animals, as well as the people, that keep me company'. At the same time, however, he has a suspicion that he never will belong properly, being 'too hasty and busy and human'. This lack of confidence in his humanity, however, is seldom found in North American writing and Laurie Kutchens is typical when she presents the human and the natural as two sides of the one reality: 'My body knows it is a landscape, capable of invitations and invasions, seduction and violation ...And I know the landscape as a body.'

This assurance gave rise to Whitman's 'barbaric yawp' which has seldom been replicated in Australian writing, Les Murray perhaps coming closest. It also leads to the optimism running through most of the North American essays which culminates in Terry Tempest Williams' dream that this communion between human beings and the natural world will put and end to 'the constraints of [the] own self-imposed structures' of a mechanistic culture and 'give birth to new institutions...[and] overhaul our religious, political and educational systems that are no longer working for us.' There is little of this utopian enthusiasm in Australian nature writing, however, rather a stoic sense that a long haul lies ahead and that the land has many demands to make upon us.

No doubt this reflects the dominant note of our culture which tends to be skeptical and utilitarian, and helps to explain why there is a certain defensiveness about many of these essays. Nevertheless they are part of a continuing tradition, what Judith Wright has called 'the inner argument between the transplanted European and his new country' or what Christopher Brennan in more exalted mode characterised as the attempt on the one hand to shape 'the world to harmony with our thought and [permeate] every corner of it with humanity and meaning' and on the other to let 'the vast region of the unconscious or subconscious' become conscious, to let the world speak in us.

This also happens to be the task which Mircea Eliade saw as essential for any settler society, the transformation of the apparent chaos before them into cosmos, into a world in which they are imaginatively at home. But there is a good deal of evidence today, in the environmental crisis facing us and in our relations with Aboriginal Australia, to suggest that the task is still unfinished, perhaps barely begun. As Patrick Dodson has said, speaking from his side of the frontier, 'Many Australians don't know how to think themselves into the country, the land. They find it hard to think with the land. We Aboriginal people find it hard to think without the land.'

If this is so then the Australian essays will demand a different reading from local readers that the North American ones do. Standing in the tradition of Thoreau and Whitman in the nineteenth century and Annie Dillard—curiously omitted from this anthology—Barry Lopez, Gary Snyder and others in the twentieth century, they come with a kind of literary imprimatur which may distance them, perhaps even turn them into what Simone de Beauvoir in one of her irreverent moments called a mere 'work of art...a statue dying of boredom in some villa garden'. The Australian essays, however, have an immediacy which bears heavily and quite explicitly on the way we imagine ourselves and our society and have palpable designs on the reader, even perhaps on the way we vote.

But that is not to denigrate them. They offer also many aesthetic pleasures. Barbara Blackman's essay, for example, offers an account of the landscape of the blind in which place, decomposed of visual substance, is left fallow to fructify again with intimations from all the other senses, some not easily imagined by those whose perceptions depend so much on sight: as in the translation of poetry, the original words divest their attaching atmospheres to be released into the different atmosphere of another language.

Eric Rolls too is at his poetically practical best letting the birds he has known there define the places he has loved and Tim Winton's essay conveys his sense of the challenge the land offers, that 'something truly sacred will eventually demand something of us, something deeper that the credit card' in a voice that is engagingly and often wittily colloquial.

Other essays refreshingly undermine many of the traditional cliches of Australian nature writing. Tom Griffiths' 'Cooper Dreaming' and Charmian Clift's 'The Centre', for example, take us to a different kind of Centre. Griffiths insists on its abundance and writes about the fruitful alliance that has been built up between pastoralists, greenies and some Aboriginal people in the Channel country to preserve that abundance and protect it from the irrigation demanded by cotton farmers elsewhere—in effect disarmingly challenging the worship of economic growth. For her part Clift—at her most exuberant here—turns an ironic eye on the image of the 'heroic bushmen', describing them in an Alice Springs pub leaning against the bar, 'authentically themselves in jeans and battered drovers' hats, so weathered, leathered, creased and sun-cured, so thirsty, exuberant, excited and vocal, that you can't quite believe in them'. The pioneering myth is also in her sights as she compares the early explorers to 'maddened lice crawling across the country' setting in train the dispossession of its Aboriginal peoples with whom she sympathises, 'the disinherited, stripped of ancient dignity, ...aimlessly drunk' in the streets outside the pub.

One of the most engaging qualities of these essays then is their variety and authenticity of style, the way the voices that speak in them sound authentically 'Australian'—whatever that may mean. But they also uniquely personal. Pete Hay's essay, 'The Red Steer At Rat Bay' is a good example. Writing about being torn between head and heart, between the officially prescribed ways of land management and fire prevention on his property and traditional Aboriginal ways, he comes to a self-ironic conclusion, that his defiance of current scientific wisdom is 'bizarre, incomprehensible' to most people but it is what he chooses. Moreover, he believes that 'I am assuredly not alone, that 'throughout the Australian bush other people, motivated by a deep biophilia, and armed with noting more tangible than love, are undertaking bush stewardship roles for which they are blissfully inadequate.'

Tim Winton, to refer to him again, turns his irony on a culture in which 'nothing is sacred but the desire to have all the toys' and on sentimental attitudes to the 'great outdoors':

> Like the kids they once were, Australians bolt for the outdoors the moment the bell goes. They stream out in hordes and stomp on the bits they can't drive over. They try to catch the light on the stones, the lorikeets in trees, with their disposable cameras and fill albums with the results while planning the next excursion.

Other essays address themselves more directly to the legacy of the idea of *terra nullius*, the way those in charge of the first settlement saw the land as an empty stage on which to play out the imperial drama of conquest and possession and to build 'a new Britannia in another world', impose their designs and names upon it. Interrogating this accepted wisdom, the notion that 'Australia' began in 1788 and that the land exists to be developed for economic profit, however, can be a tricky business, as current controversies over indigenous rights and attitudes to land suggest. So the essays which broach the subject do so tactfully, aware no doubt that environmentalists are often seen as 'nutters' and somehow 'un-Australian' and one must admire their skill.

John Cameron's essay, for instance, begins engagingly with memories of being a 'teenage rockhound growing up in Canberra', then moves to his subsequent interest in geology which enables him to explore links between the present city and its past and thus to include the Aboriginal story. Others like William Lines steer even further away from New Age romanticism, insisting on the physical actuality of the place, the 'sun blasted world' of his childhood to which he only felt he had returned after some time away when the 'sweat ran down my forehead, across my back and under my arms'.

Overall then the Australians resist the metaphysics, what T.E. Hulme called the tendency to go 'flying up into the eternal gas', the rhapsodic note to be found in many of the North American essays. But to my taste that may be their peculiar strength in a post-modern world which, as Jean Baudrillard says, rests on 'the exaltation of signs based on the denial of the reality of things'. So the challenge to commonsense which Lines makes in his essay may be more important than it seems at first:

> Many people think of our [Australian] culture as materialistic.
> Unfortunately we do not actually value the material world for its
> own sake. We are fantasists. Most of the material objects we buy
> and consume are sold on the basis of the fantasy ascribed to them
> by advertisers.

As he goes on to point out, challenging sentimental views of their culture, 'Australian Aborigines were materialists. They knew their lives depended on an intimate acquaintance with animals, plants, water-courses, seasons and weather. They did not try to escape corporeal existence.'

To return to Chaucer's image with which we began it may sum up the situation facing Australian culture, at least as the writers here see it. Whether the North Americans have really found their way in is not for me to question.

GREG McLAREN

BEING PRECISE: POETS AND THEIR CONVICTIONS

Judith Beveridge, *Wolf Notes*, Sydney, Giramondo, 2003
Anthony Lawrence, *The Sleep of a Learning Man*, Sydney, Giramondo, 2003

The first thing I noticed when looking at these two collections was the attractiveness of their design and layout, maintaining a standard set by the prior publications by Giramondo. Ivor Indyk and Evelyn Juers' new press has quickly filled the gap in poetry publishing opened up by the recent absence of Paper Bark Press. With the addition of Giramondo and another impressive new press, Salt, to the more established houses like University of Queensland Press, Fremantle Arts Centre Press, Brandl & Schlesinger, Black Pepper, and Penguin's occasional forays into poetry, Australian poets and poetry readers are relatively well-served compared to the situation as it appeared just a few short years ago.

I found this new collection by Anthony Lawrence a troubling one. It is beset with a troubling mixture of a small amount of very powerful work indeed alongside many poems hobbled by what seems to be deep self-regard. Nearly everything in Lawrence's work, it sometimes seems, comes back to Lawrence's role as "poet", a tendency Judith Beveridge identified in her review (*HEAT* 10 [1998]) of Lawrence's *New and Selected Poems*. In "Hill End, 1963", the events in the poem are reduced to a literary residue: and "I return to my body with the makings of new poetry". Lawrence finds poetry and language as his only response to a fishing expedition in "Woodbridge":

> I want to read them a Lorca poem—
> something about how, in a certain light,
> a woman's thighs can be like a school
> of minnows...

In an otherwise impressive poem like "The Cryptographs of the Head", Lawrence again places language and poetry as a mediating tissue between himself and the world. The more Lawrence tries to reify himself, the more distantly the possibility of his joining with the world, or other people, or even, it seems, his own experience, in an unself-conscious manner recedes. Even in these poems of the natural world, or in those about other people, the poems very often reflect attention back to Lawrence's self-awareness as a poet. It is as if this is the default setting of Lawrence's sensibility. Such an effect begins to jar, and then to grate, very quickly, and it occurs in poem after poem throughout the collection.

Similarly, Lawrence places himself at the centre of poems that ostensibly point at other subject matter. In "Owls", the dead bird's "blood smells like a memory of wet birds", returning us again to Lawrence's speaker's psyche. The final lines of this poem point out an alienation from the natural world that is strange, given Lawrence's anxiety in his poetry to be part of that world:

> Moonlight seems to amplify my wrist blood
> dropping to a carpet of needles.
> It could be the sound of a barn owl blinking.

Lawrence seems hardly able to write about something without relating it to himself in some way. The correspondences Lawrence sees between himself and the natural world often seem forced, even contrived: they don't always seem to arise out of the image or anecdote. He rarely speaks of things' connections to each other, but more typically of their connection to him, or connected to each other through Lawrence, as if meaning radiates out from Lawrence's own centre.

What is most troubling in this book is that even in otherwise delicately strong poems, Lawrence's poet-consciousness and self-regard remains present. "Two Poems I" is moving, but this quality is compromised by Lawrence's self-conscious mannerisms. He writes of friends who have died, intimating that

> I am being precise
> because I am listening to James Wright
> who loved to name and count things.

And, at the poem's end:

> I know this
> because James Wright's voice is already bleak
> with dying.

This poem detracts from his friend's death and the grief of the "seven schoolgirls" also mourning her, and focuses instead on Lawrence's reading of other poets: again foregrounding Lawrence's status as "poet". It is as if Lawrence feels he has no option but to mediate experience and feeling with poetry, as if poetry and poetry only validates experience.

The stand-out poems in *The Sleep of a Learning Man*, for me, are the gruelling "The Language of Bleak Averages" and "The Extended Narrative of Their Lives". In the former, although Lawrence remains a prominent feature of the poem, he plots out the emotional toll in a matter-of-fact way that does not draw attention to himself. The poem instead acts like "graphs of emotion", as Phillip Hodgins put it in "Kitchen" from *Things Happen*. In this, Lawrence is at once understated and brutally plain. That he retains this capacity, to appall without also self-aggrandising, is both a positive sign for Lawrence's future work, but disappointing in terms of the collection as a whole. This facility is very largely absent from the other poems here.

"The Extended Narrative of Their Lives" is a powerful poem, but unfortunately does not escape Lawrence's poeticising. There are grating similes like this:

> The shadow of a Mason's handshake
> the colour of a rusted service revolver
> fell across my grandfather's grave.

There is too much attention here given to Lawrence's facility with image-making: the reader certainly notices Lawrence's simile, but could almost forget it is a description of a funeral. There seems no reason for Lawrence to shift attention from the grandfather's funeral to his own apparent skill as a poet. Again, Lawrence's seeming inability to restrain his image-making comes to the fore in self-conscious "literary" phrases like "cursives of marram grass", "words surfaced, knotted,/ like an ampersand at his lips". Lawrence is much more evocative in this setting at least when using a more direct image: "When the minister palmed a clod to the wood,/ I heard a single doorknock". While these poems represent what is best about Lawrence's work, in *The Sleep of a Learning Man*, at best he seems, unfortunately to be treading water. The gulf between poems of this sort and much of the rest of the book is such that at times it seems as if Lawrence is two different poets. This is a quite serious tension he needs to resolve.

In his recent review of Judith Beveridge's *Wolf Notes*, Peter Pierce barely touches on a major driving force behind Beveridge's work: her interest in Buddhism. He writes only that Beveridge "has put her craft bravely at the service of her convictions" (*Sydney Morning Herald*, June 12–13, 2004, *Spectrum*, p. 12). This is a quite inadequate summation of the religious impetus behind "From the Palace to the Bodhi Tree", a long sequence written in the voice of Siddhattha Gotama, the future Buddha, prior to his enlightenment. This sequence is not only the centre-piece of Beveridge's new collection but is also Beveridge's single most significant work to date, and deserves the greater share of attention in any critical response to this book.

Beveridge plots Siddhattha's ascetic and spiritual practices as he edges closer to what we now know as Buddhism. She empties out and restrains some of her trademark poetics in order to allow the narrative to dominate. Beveridge allows Siddhattha to speak for himself, edging through the narrative without any doctrinal commentary of note. She shows us Siddhattha as he slowly discovers a non-attached perspective in "Quarry":

> I let go of all thought—
> and I felt like a bird
> floating in the clear, excavated air
>
> high above the talus.

Siddhattha acts with an increasingly radical humility in "In the Forest":

> All day I bow to these creatures –
> those who wait their cycles out more
>
> devoutly than moons.

Interspersed with poems that are obviously concerned with plotting Siddhattha's geographical and spiritual wandering is a series of vows in poems such as "Vow", "A Vow" and "Eight Gathas". These map a steady shift in Siddhattha's outlook until he makes the ultimate vow of empathy, non-attachment and no-self in "Ficus Religiosa":

Under the tree pressing me into its embrace—
I vow with all beings
to sit until I no longer want
to burgeon in paradise.

The sequence does not work solely, though, on a straight, dramatic narrative plane. Beveridge understands that there are significant elements of Siddhattha's story which cannot be represented directly by narrative means. The technical reach of this sequence in this regard is really quite impressive but subtle. As Siddhattha nears enlightenment, Beveridge's formal poetics become more structured and complex. She manages this shift in such a way as to evoke Siddhattha's approach to his enlightenment. Beveridge's use of the sonnet form in "Rice" is particularly astute. Siddhattha's realisation about *dukkha*, suffering brought about by craving and attachment, pivots on that form's conventional turn between the octave and the sestet. This provides a very neat but barely noticeable integration of the qualities of a traditional English poetic form in the service of a narrative drawn from an "Asian" spiritual tradition. This integration is a mark of Beveridge's poetry generally, but has reached something of a peak in this collection. Although the sequence may be a little over-long for some readers, for those familiar with the story of Siddhattha, it rewards re-reading many times over.

The strength of this book is also its weakness. The central sequence does depend somewhat on the reader's interest in the story of Siddhattha Gotama prior to his attaining Buddhahood. While a handful of the poems in the over fifty pages of "From the Palace to the Bodhi Tree" do not impel the narrative in any significant way. While these poems ("Horse", "Buffalos", "Tigers", "Snake", "Dark Night", "Four Summer Fragments") do look to be superfluous to the sequence's narrative, even these provide some element of texture that adds to the depth and weight of recurrent images that form a network of motifs that hold the sequence together aesthetically.

The other two sections of *Wolf Notes*, "Peregrine" and "Signatures", contain what are largely developments of other strands of Beveridge's work. Many of the poems in "Peregrine", such as "Bahadour", "The Saffron Picker", "The Dice-Player", "The Pedlar", "The Bone Artisan" return to poems from Beveridge's last book, *Accidental Grace*, that were set in India. This section reflects a sense of the comic in Beveridge's work that has previously been less apparent.

Beveridge's punning in "The Bone Artisan" in particular adds a lightness of tone, but the sense of play is at a peak in "Dog Divinations", drawn in part from the ancient Indian dog prophecy text, the *Sarngadhara Paddhati*. This poem reads as an esoteric counterpart to poems from *Accidental Grace* like "How to Love Bats" and "How to Love Snakes", and the strand of poetry in Beveridge's work that displays such empathy with and concern for the natural world: apparently,

> If a dog defecates
>
> after digging on the upper side of a house, then the mistress's paramour is on his way...

The majority of poems in "Signatures" are just that: monologues spoken from the perspective of characters engaged in a range of occupations. This continues Beveridge's interest in writing in voices other than her own: "Apprentice", "An Artist Speaks to his Model", "Sailor", "The Courtesan" all proceed with intimate but varied voices. Beveridge's shifting of voice and perspective is not only related to her Buddhist interests, but also signals a commitment to a continual stretching of her poetic range. While Beveridge takes nothing in her work for granted, in *The Sleep of a Learning Man*, Anthony Lawrence seems relatively complacent. It will be interesting to see how both these poets respond in subsequent volumes to the challenges of technique and subject matter they have wittingly or otherwise set themselves.

Readers of *Southerly*
are invited to become
members of

The English Association, Sydney

Southerly is the journal of The English Association
and members receive three issues of the journal each
year.

By becoming a member of The English Association you
will also be supporting the activities of the Association
in promoting English at school and university level. These
activities include running conferences for
teachers and students of HSC English.

To inquire about membership of The English Association
please copy the form on the next page, fill out the details
and post it to:

The English Association, Sydney
Box 91 Wentworth Building
University of Sydney NSW 2006

NOTES ON CONTRIBUTORS

ROBERT ADAMSON is the author of several collections of poetry and prose. His latest is an autobiography entitled *Inside Out*.

JUDITH BEVERIDGE is a widely admired poet and teacher of creative writing. Her latest collection is *Wolf Notes*.

VERONICA BRADY, an internationally known speaker and Catholic activist, is the author of many books including the biography of Judith Wright, *South of My Days*.

COLLEEN Z BURKE'S new poetry collection, *The Odd Pagan or Two* is due out in 2004. She's also co-editor of *The Turning Wave: Poems and Songs of Irish Australia*.

JOHN I. CAMERON is a Senior Lecturer in Social Ecology at the University of Western Sydney with a background is Geology and Environmental Economics. He is the editor of *Changing Places: Reimagining Sense of Place in Australia*, a volume of writings from the colloquia.

LIANA JOY CHRISTENSEN teaches at Murdoch University. She was editor of *Landscope* magazine for its first five years, and has published poetry, essays and articles on environmental themes.

LOUISE CRISP lives in rural Victoria. Her latest collection is *Ruby Camp: A Snowy River Series*.

NICK DRAYSON is the recent winner of the inaugural WILDCARE Tasmania Nature Writing Prize. He has worked as a newspaper journalist and freelance writer for publications such as the Australian Geographic. His first novel, *Confessing a Murder*, was published in 2002.

ROBERT GRAY is a prizewinning poet. His latest collection is *New Selected Poems*. He is currently working on an autobiography.

TOM GRIFFITHS is a Senior Fellow in the History Program of the Research School of Social Sciences at the Australian National University. His latest book, *Hunters and Collectors* (1996) was awarded numerous prestigious prizes.

JENNIFER HARRISON'S latest collection is *Dear B*. She recently co-edited the Melbourne anthology *Said The Rat!* for the Fellowship of Australian Writers and has a new collection of poetry forthcoming from Black Pepper Press. In 2003 she won the NSW Women Writers' National Poetry Prize.

MARTIN HARRISON teaches Creative Writing at the University of Technology, Sydney and is the author of *Summer* (Paperbark 2002).

DINAH HAWKEN a New Zealand poet. She also convenes a workshop in environmental writing at the International Institute of Modern Letters at Victoria University.

PETER HAY is Reader in Geography and Environmental Studies at the University of Tasmania. His works include a collection of poetry, *The View from the Non-Members Bar* and *Main Currents in Western Environmental Thought*.

BARBARA HOLLOWAY is a Canberra writer who "interviewed" Dame Mary Gilmore for the ANU's TV Environment Series, "Ten Green Bottles".

JOHN HUGHES is an essayist and playwright. His most recent publication is *The Idea of Home* (Giramondo, 2004).

CHRISTOPHER KELEN is a poet currently living in Hong Kong.

LAURIE KUTCHINS is Associate Professor of Creative Writing at James Madison University (USA), and has spent the last two years as a visiting writer at the University of New. Her latest collection is *The Night Path*.

ANTHONY LAWRENCE latest collection is *The Sleep of a Learning Man*. He lives in Tasmania.

ILINDA MARKOVA is originally from Bulgaria. She is a poet playwright and screenwriter.

PETER MINTER'S collection *Empty Texas* was a co-winner of the Age Book of the Year. He works in the Koori Centre at the University of Sydney.

DAVID PRATER is the editor of the literary journal *Cordite*. His poetry is widely published in Australia and overseas.

KATE RIGBY is a Senior Lecturer in German Studies and Comparative Literature at Monash University. She has published books and articles on German literature, feminist theory, ecocriticism and ecophilosophy, and is the co-editor of PAN (Philosophy Activism Nature).

ERIC ROLLS latest book is *Australia: a biography Volume 2*. He is a member of the Order of Australia (AM) for services to literature and environmental awareness in 1992 and was awarded a Doctor of the University, University of Canberra in 1995. He is a Fellow of the Australian Academy of the Humanities.

MICAELA SAHAR lives in Melbourne but writes everywhere, collecting words carefully.

NONIE SHARP has worked with north Australia's indigenous coastal peoples for 25 years. Her most recent book, *Saltwater People: The Waves of Memory*. She is currently completing a five-year Australian Research Fellowship at La Trobe University.

Scott Slovic is the Professor of Literature and the Environment at the University of Nevada. Author and editor of many works on the environment, he is currently working on an anthology of Australian desert literature.

Margaret Sommerville's *Wildflowering: The Life and Places of Kathleen McArthur* is forthcoming this year.

Nicolette Stasko is a prize-winning poet whose latest book is *The Weight of Irises*. She is the author of *Oyster: From Montparnasse to Greenwell Point*.

Mark Tredinnick is an essayist and writing teacher. He has just finished his landscape memoir, *The Blue Plateau: A Natural History of Home*. His book *The Wild Music* will appear late in 2005. Mark is the editor of *A Place on Earth* (2003), an anthology of Australian and US nature writing.

Elaine Van Kempen is one of the original conveners of Watermark, a bi-annual celebration of nature writing.

Charlie Ward is a member of the Daguragu Council. He lives in outback Northern territory.

Herb Wharton began his working life in his teenage years as drover. His books include *Where Ya' Been, Mate?* and *Cattle Camp*, a collection of short stories. He was the first Aboriginal artist to enjoy a residency at the Australia Council studio at the Cite des Arts and was awarded a Centenary Medal for services to indigenous literature.

John Wolsey is an artist living in Whipstick Forest near Bendigo. He has recently won the NSW Art Gallery's Wynne Waterston Prize for his painting, "Rare and Unsuspected Sightings of the Embroidered Merops & Spinifex Grass".

Petra White was born in Adelaide and has been living and writing in Melbourne forsix years She has recently completed Honours in English at Melbourne University.

Ouyang Yu is well known for his poetry, translations and the novel *The Eastern Slope Chronicle*. He also edits *Otherland*, a bilingual journal of Chinese and Australian writing.